RELEASED

THE DECLINE OF THE CHARTIST MOVEMENT

ST. JOSEPH'S UNIVERSITY   STX
HD8396.S55 1968
The decline of the Chartist movement.

3 9353 00088 3973

BY

PRESTON WILLIAM SLOSSON

HD
8396
S55
1968

AMS PRESS
NEW YORK

123532

COLUMBIA UNIVERSITY
STUDIES IN THE
SOCIAL SCIENCES

172

The Series was formerly known as
Studies in History, Economics and Public Law.

Reprinted with the permission of Columbia University Press
From the edition of 1916, New York
First AMS EDITION published 1968
Manufactured in the United States of America

Library of Congress Catalogue Card Number: 74-76700

AMS PRESS, INC.
NEW YORK, N. Y. 10003

PREFACE

THE present study is rather a problem in causation than a complete narrative of the Chartist movement. During a score of years, which may be roughly indicated as lying between the Poor Law Amendment Act of 1834 and the outbreak of the Crimean War, the portion of the British laboring classes which aspired to play a part in national politics entered the political arena not as an ally of the middle-class reformers but as an independent party with a program and an organization of its own. Ever since that time many individuals have preached class-consciousness to the workers, but it was not until the recent organization of the Labour Party that a political party based upon class lines was again able to win the allegiance of a majority or even a large minority of British workingmen. Even the present-day Labour Party has been less independent of the Liberals than were the Chartists, although this may be due rather to the necessary compromises of Parliamentary work than to lack of class feeling. Why a popular movement, so generally supported by the unenfranchised classes of Great Britain as was the Chartist agitation, should have been abandoned without attaining the program of reforms to which it was pledged is a difficult and complex question and one to which insufficient attention has been paid. The aim of the present survey has been to contribute a little to the discussion of this vitally important question in the political history of Great Britain in the nineteenth century.

The writer owes much to the Columbia School of Political Science for instruction and inspiration, but an especial debt

5

of gratitude to Professor James T. Shotwell for taking this study in charge; to Professor Carlton Hayes and to Professor William Archibald Dunning for the time and attention which they have so freely given to supervising its preparation; to Professor Edwin R. A. Seligman for generously granting access to the remarkable collection of source material for British social history in his library; to Mr. Edward A. Porritt, author of *The Unreformed House of Commons*, for helpful suggestions; and to Mr. J. H. Park, whose forthcoming study of *The Reform Bill of 1867* adds to this another chapter in the struggle for the reform of the British franchise.

PRESTON WILLIAM SLOSSON.

MAY, 1916.

CONTENTS

CHAPTER I

CHARTISM AS A CLASS MOVEMENT

CHAPTER II

THE HIGH TIDE OF CHARTISM

8   *CONTENTS*   **[256**

CHAPTER III

THE DISINTEGRATION OF THE CHARTIST MOVEMENT

CHAPTER IV

THE IMPROVEMENT IN THE CONDITION OF THE BRITISH WORKING CLASS AFTER 1842

CHAPTER V

A DISCUSSION OF THE CAUSES OF THE DECLINE OF THE CHARTIST MOVEMENT

CHAPTER VI

THE RESPONSE OF THE RULING CLASSES OF GREAT BRITAIN TO THE CHARTIST MOVEMENT

CHAPTER VII

THE PERMANENT INFLUENCE OF CHARTISM ON THE BRITISH WORKING CLASS

INTRODUCTION

THE six demands of the People's Charter: manhood suffrage, equal election districts, annual Parliaments, abolition of the property qualification for members of the House of Commons, vote by ballot, and salaries for members of Parliament, had all been long familiar to British reformers before they attained such a degree of popular support as makes it possible for us to speak of a Chartist *movement*. The Chartists themselves claimed that their aim was but to restore the ancient constitution of England as it existed prior to the rise of the centralized Tudor monarchy. History does not justify their faith, but dates the Charter as a political demand from the latter part of the eighteenth century. Major John Cartwright urged four of its six points in 1776, and Charles James Fox later advocated them all. Even the name "Charter" for a political program was no novelty. A pamphlet of 1832, entitled *The People's Charter*,[1] besides recommending such political reforms as universal suffrage, vote by ballot and annual Parliaments, advocated numerous other reforms which it assumed would result from political democracy, such as an untaxed press, factory legislation, a militia instead of a standing army, abolition of the kingship, and the further abolition of numerous abuses; such as, sinecures and high salaries, the established church, the bank monopoly, primogeniture, the corn laws, the poor laws, West Indian slavery, the national debt, the peerage, the game laws, imprisonment for debt,

---

[1] *The People's Charter*, an abstract from *The Rights of Nations* (London, 1832).

and all taxes except a graduated property tax. All of these aims were congenial to the Chartists, but it seems, on the whole, that the date of this pamphlet is more significant than its title. It did not clearly recommend all of the six points of Chartism and its elaborate detail is characteristic of the doctrinaire radicalism of the years before the Reform Act of 1832.

The germ of the Chartist party was the London Workingmen's Association, under the able leadership of William Lovett. While the phrasing of the People's Charter varied somewhat at different periods, the text of the 1837 petition of the London Workingmen's Association [1] is typical of later forms:

Equal Representation. That the United Kingdom be divided into 200 electoral districts, dividing as nearly as possible an equal number of inhabitants; and that each district do send a representative to Parliament.

Universal Suffrage. That every person producing proofs of his being 21 years of age to the clerk of the parish in which he has resided for six months, shall be entitled to have his name registered as a voter. That the time for registering in each year be from the 1st of January to the 1st of March.

Annual Parliament. That a general election do take place on the 24th of June in each year, and that each vacancy be filled up a fortnight after it occurs. That the hours of voting be from six o'clock in the morning till six o'clock in the evening.

No Property Qualifications. That there shall be no property qualifications for members; but on a requisition signed by 200 voters, in favour of any candidate, being presented to the clerk of the parish in which they reside, such candidate shall be put in nomination. And a list of all the candidates nominated throughout the district shall be stuck on the church door in every parish, to enable voters to judge of their qualifications.

[1] *Bronterre's National Reformer*, Feb. 11, 1837.

Vote by Ballot. That each voter must vote in the parish in which he resides. That each parish provide as many balloting boxes as there are candidates proposed in the district, and that a temporary place be fitted up in each parish church for the purpose of secret voting. And on the day of election, as each voter passes orderly on to the ballot, he shall have given to him by the officer in attendance, a ballotting ball which he shall drop into the box of his favorite candidate. At the close of the day the votes shall be counted by the proper officers, and the numbers stuck on the church doors. The following day the clerk of the district and two examiners shall collect the votes of all the parishes throughout the district, and cause the name of the successful candidate to be posted in every parish of the district.

Sittings and Payments to Members. That the members do take their seats in Parliament on the first Monday in October, next after their election, and continue their sittings every day (Sundays excepted) till the business of the sitting is terminated, but not later than the first of September. They shall meet every day (during the session) for business at ten o'clock in the morning, and adjourn at four. And every member shall be paid (quarterly) out of the public treasury £400 a year.

That all electoral officers be elected by universal suffrage.

It will be seen that had the Charter become the law of the land several incidental reforms would have been accomplished as well as the six points; such as the abolition of plural voting, nominations by popular petition, a decrease in the size of the House of Commons and a mandatory working week for the representatives of the people. In 1839 [1] the Chartist proposal increased the number of electoral districts to three hundred and the remuneration of members of Parliament to £500 a year. But no important change was ever made in the Charter except that whereas

---

[1] *Chartist Circular,* Oct. 5, 1839.

during the first two or three years of the movement it was customary to speak of the "five points," neglecting the question of equal electoral districts,[1] during the period covered by this study the word "Charter" invariably stood for all six of the fundamental reforms of the party.

Besides the text of the Charter itself, and the various preambles to the successive petitions to the House of Commons consisting for the most part of surveys of popular grievances, the best primary records of Chartism are the pamphlets and newspapers of the party. Over fifty Chartist pamphlets are listed in Gotthilf Dierlamm's *Die Flugschrif-tenliteratur der Chartistenbewegung* (Naumburg, 1909); over sixty periodicals more or less Chartist are given in R. G. Gammage's *History of the Chartist Movement* (London, 1894) or in other secondary sources. The non-Chartist press devoted no little attention to the movement, and a fairly complete—if not altogether unbiassed—history of Chartism could be compiled from the London *Times*, the *Annual Register*, Hansard's *Parliamentary Debates* and similar external sources without any reference to Chartist authorities. The memoirs or miscellaneous writings of the Chartist leaders, such as William Lovett, Thomas Cooper, J. Bronterre O'Brien, G. J. Holyoake, S. B. Bamford, W. J. Linton and many others, are of course of great value; but it should always be remembered in reading them that no movement was ever more torn by faction and internal strife than the Chartist, and that it is in consequence hopeless to seek a quite unprejudiced criticism of men and events. Valuable sidelights are thrown upon the course of the movement by the writings of sympathetic contemporary observers, such as Charles Kingsley, Benjamin Disraeli, Thomas Carlyle, Karl Marx and Friedrich Engels.

[1] The prayer of the petition of 1839 as given in *Hansard*, 3d series, vol. xlviii, p. 227, does not mention equal electoral districts.

We are not so well off for secondary sources of Chartist history as for primary. R. G. Gammage's *History of the Chartist Movement* is indeed the one book which is indispensable to every student of the movement, as much so to-day as when it was written in 1854. This is not only because it is a full and well-considered outline of the actual events of the movement, not only because of much valuable information assembled by the author, but because Gammage was one of the party leaders and so was possessed of much inside information which is unobtainable elsewhere. But Gammage's book is not impeccable. The 1894 edition contains letters by his fellow Chartists Thomas Cooper and William Ryder correcting errors in his account, and the author acknowledges the justice of many of their corrections. In the *Life of Thomas Cooper*, by Himself (London, 1872), Cooper criticizes Gammage's *History* yet further, adding, however, the consolatory remark (true even today) that " I know no person living who could write a History of Chartism without making mistakes." [1] More important than a few minor and inevitable misstatements is the strong partisan bias which Gammage shows on every page, though to no greater a degree than other Chartists. But the chief reason for regarding his work rather as a valuable source than as a satisfactory history is that while an admirable chronicle it is nothing more; it does not give that economic background which is essential to any understanding of the causes of events. Many brief and well-balanced incidental accounts of Chartism occur in general histories, such as W. M. Molesworth's *A History of England from the Year 1830* (London, 1872), vol. ii; H. M. Hyndman's *The Historical Basis of Socialism in England* (London, 1883), and, the best of all perhaps, *The Rise of Democracy*, by J. Holland Rose (London, 1897).

[1] *Life of Thomas Cooper*, p. 278.

Although Chartism was a purely British movement, the student will find secondary material comparatively abundant in languages other than English, particularly in German. The best and fullest account of the Chartist movement as a whole and also of many of its special phases, such as its relation to the feminist movement, is to be found in Hermann Schlüter's *Die Chartisten-Bewegung* (New York, 1916). This work, which is an elaboration of *Die Chartistenbewegung in England* in the *Sozial-Demokratische Bibliothek*, vol. xvi (Zürich, 1887), is written entirely from the standpoint of orthodox Marxian Socialism. Its only rival for completeness and scope is *Le Chartisme,* by Édouard Dolléans (Paris, 1912), which is in two volumes and contains over nine hundred pages. This work is rather vague and diffuse, and, while it quotes freely, lacks a bibliography. In German we have also a very valuable study of the origins of the movement in *Die Entstehung und die Okonomischen Grundsätze der Chartistenbewegung*, by Dr. John L. Tildsley (Jena, 1898); also *Die Flugschriftenliteratur der Chartistenbewegung, op. cit.*, based in part on Dr. Tildsley's work, and *Die Englische Chartistenbewegung*, by Lujo Brentano, *Preussische Jahrbücher*, vol. xxxiii (Berlin, 1874). In Russian there is a brief account, *Chartistskoe dvizhenie*, by N. B. Krichevski (St. Petersburg, 1906).

CHAPTER I

CHARTISM AS A CLASS MOVEMENT

CHARTISM may be briefly defined as that phase of the movement for political democracy in Great Britain which centered its hopes upon the six principles of the People's Charter: manhood suffrage, equal election districts, annual Parliaments, abolition of the property qualification for membership in the House of Commons, vote by ballot, and payment for members of Parliament. The Charter was but one of many radically democratic programs which were proposed during the second quarter of the nineteenth century, but it was the only one to find general support among the still unenfranchised classes. The aim of each of the points of the Charter was to win for these classes a majority in the House of Commons; for it was believed that control of the House of Commons implied control of the government, and that the king and the House of Lords could no more resist a working-class majority in the lower house than they had been able to resist the majority of middle-class reformers in that house in 1832.

Prior to the Reform Bill of 1832, the British working classes had never entered politics as a separate party. The violence of the Luddite machine wreckers, the growth of trades unions and the prevalence of strikes indicated, indeed, the sharpest conflict between manufacturers and operatives in the economic field, but both joined forces to attack the virtual monopoly of power enjoyed by the landlord class. In 1832, there were two main political groups in Great Britain, the reformers, including both the Whigs and the Radicals, and the anti-reformers, or Tories. But the victory of reform was followed by the division of the reformers into factions. The Whigs, or ministerialists, opposed further political change, at least until the country should have fully recovered from its years of agitation. The Radicals desired extensive changes in the civil and criminal law; the abolition of special privileges, such as the Anglican Church enjoyed; complete free trade, and an immediate extension of the franchise. Most of the Radicals favored household suffrage, the ballot, abolition of the property qualification for the House of Commons, and shorter sessions of Parliament; some of them favored every point of the Charter. They were not sufficiently numerous in the House of Commons to form a ministry or even to organize as a formally separate party, but they criticized the government freely, contested Whig seats at elections, and frequently voted against the ministry on crucial divisions. Their influence was far out of proportion to their numbers, for their leaders included some of the ablest men in Parliament, and had, besides, the moral weight of a widespread popular support.

Before the meeting of the reformed Parliament the Radicals had not regarded themselves nor were they regarded by the people as primarily representatives of the middle classes. They were rather considered as the champions of popular rights and the expounders of popular grievances in general; their political and economic policies were understood to favor the interests of the laborers as well as manufacturing and commercial interests. Some of the earlier Radicals, indeed, specialized in reforms of interest to the working classes. Francis Place, for example, devoted himself chiefly to securing liberty for the trades unions. William Cobbett, one of the older generation of reformers, although new to Parliament, vigorously opposed the Poor Law Amendment Act of 1834.[1] But the Radical leaders most prominent during the period of Chartist activity, Bright, Cobden, Hume, Roebuck and Lord Brougham, were regarded with growing dislike and disfavor by many of the artisans, while retaining the confidence of a large proportion of the middle classes. There were two main causes for this growing political opposition between the working classes and their employers: the fact that the Reform Bill greatly increased the opportunity of the middle classes to obtain representation in Parliament, while leaving the workers practically without direct influence upon the parties in the House of Commons; and the entrance of economic issues, upon which the interests of the two classes were opposed, into the sphere of practical politics. The masses of the people found that the Radicals were no longer representing them, and their discontent continued to grow until it ripened at last into the Chartist movement.

The Chartists, unlike the Radicals, must be reckoned not only a separate political group but a separate political party. They stood quite independent of the Whig and Tory organizations and maintained party machinery of their own. The general policies and tactics of the party were determined in conventions of delegates chosen by local Chartist associations, and their execution was left to a permanent executive committee and to paid lecturers and propagandist agents. The organization was the product of a merger between the London Working Men's Association, led by William Lovett and Henry Vincent; the Birmingham Political Union, including Thomas Atwood and John Collins; and the political unions organized by Feargus

---

[1] *Cf. infra*, p. 57.

O'Connor.[1] In 1840, these organizations took the common name of the National Charter Association. Any person taking out a card of membership, renewable quarterly for the nominal fee of twopence, was admitted. The executive, elected by the whole membership of the association, consisted of a secretary, a treasurer, and five other members. The secretary and the treasurer each received two pounds a week for their services, and the other members thirty shillings a week during their sittings. The executive had at its disposal half the funds of the association.[2] Of the many alternative forms of party organization proposed, perhaps the most interesting was that by Dr. McDouall, who suggested in 1841 [3] the organization of the party by trades. There should be, for example, a Shoemakers' Chartist Association, not identified with any trade union but representing the political interests of the shoemakers as an industry.

The separate party existence of the Chartists is often ignored because they were practically without representation in Parliament.[4] Yet the movement absorbed the larger part of the politically active working class which had given invaluable support to the agitation for reform. The Chartists could not consistently support the Whig ministry, since it was opposed to further popular agitation, but the Radicals would have welcomed the aid of a politically active working class which, even unenfranchised, would have lent weight to their demands. If the Radicals had not lost the confidence of the British working classes there might never

---

[1] Gammage, *History of the Chartist Movement*, p. 15.

[2] *Ibid.*, pp. 183-4.

[3] *English Chartist Circular*, vol. i, pp. 57-8.

[4] Many of the Radicals in Parliament, however, were in sympathy with the Charter, and some of them, such as Thomas Duncombe, vigorously advocated it on the floor of the Commons.

have been a Chartist movement; the poverty and dissatisfaction of the people, no matter how great, would only have increased the number of unrepresented Radicals. During the decade following the Reform Bill, on the contrary, the working class drew away from their old allies and leaders, largely because of the attitude of the reformed House of Commons and even the most active of the Parliamentary reformers towards the questions of social politics which most interested the people.

The Reform Bill of 1832 was a great disappointment to Radicals and Chartists alike. At no time during the Chartist agitation did the number of electors in the counties and boroughs of England and Wales amount to one million. In 1853-4, the number of county electors was officially reckoned at 520,729; the borough electors at 430,311.[1] 363,375 electors were qualified under the ten-pound householder franchise; the rest representing older franchises. The Reform Bill not only left political power in the hands of a small minority of the nation, but superseded more democratic systems which had existed in a few of the boroughs. In the industrial borough of Preston, for example, the franchise had been extended to most of the male inhabitants[2] and the Reform Bill came there as a measure of restriction of the suffrage. Gilbert Slater is even of the opinion that as a result of these disfranchisements the proportion of British workingmen eligible to vote was smaller after 1832 than it had been before.[3] In any case, the new uniform borough constituencies were marked off from the unenfranchised by a sharper class line than ever,

---

[1] *Parliamentary Papers*, 1854 (69), liii, 219.

[2] J. McCarthy, *History of Our Own Times*, 4 vols. (London, 1880), vol. i, pp. 109-10.

[3] G. Slater, *The Making of Modern England* (Boston, 1915), p. 97.

since the new law enfranchised only the well-to-do and excluded none but the relatively poor.

Both the Radicals and the reformers who were afterwards Chartists were willing to accept the Reform Bill as an instalment of justice. But a political system which might be tolerated as temporary they regarded as unendurable if it were to be treated as a finality. Lord John Russell, as chief of the Whig ministry, during the debates on the Reform Bill made it plain that he did not expect to see any further extension of the franchise even after the victory of the Reform Bill,[1] " because both those who supported and those who opposed it were alike determined to go no further, but to use their best endeavors to preserve the renovated constitution, entire and unimpaired ". As soon as the Radicals became convinced that these words were not merely an attempt to reassure timid supporters of the measure, they accused the Whigs of betraying the democratic cause. Lord Brougham replied to Lord John Russell's defense of his course[2] by a vigorous attack in which he declared his readiness to support franchise reform " even far beyond household suffrage ".[3] But every attempt made in Parliament to alter the basis of the suffrage, to introduce the ballot or to abolish the property qualification for membership in the House of Commons met with sharp ministerial opposition and was defeated by a decisive majority.

The Chartists soon came to the conclusion that it was harder to obtain their six points from the reformed House of Commons than it would have been to win them had there been no reform at all, for the very reason advanced

---

[1] *Hansard*, 3d series, vol. xiii, p. 462.

[2] *Letter to the Electors of Stroud* (1839).

[3] *Reply to Lord John Russell's Letter to the Electors of Stroud* (1839), p. 15.

by Lord Russell that the newly enfranchised were in no hurry to share their privileges, while the opponents of reform were more than ever determined to prevent changes from extending further. In the opinion of the Chartists:

The Reform Act admitted the middle classes to a share of that power which was formerly engrossed by the aristocracy . . . but what is the consequence of the Reform Act to us, the people? Why, that the number of our opponents, of those interested to uphold the monopoly of legislative abuse, is more than doubled; and, instead of having the middle classes on our side, making common cause with us against the aristocracy, we have to contend against a combination of the aristocracy and middle order.[1]

They were resolved never to work again for any extension of the franchise short of manhood suffrage, lest they should be deceived once more by the creation of a new privileged class, the stronger because the more broadly based. In consequence they viewed the Radical efforts to obtain small concessions with positive suspicion as so many attempts to erect barriers against complete democracy. The favorite Radical franchise measure was household suffrage and this the Chartists strongly opposed. Two extracts from Chartist periodicals on this issue will serve to illustrate the general Chartist attitude towards piecemeal reform:

It is plain it would be preferable to have the old Tory system revived, to a £5 or Household Suffrage. By the former we might expect to have our ranks filled with men who, rather than have *no* extension, would demand Universal Suffrage; while, by the latter, we have the gloomy prospect of increased foes, and a decreased force to overcome them.[2]

[1] *Right and Expediency of Universal Suffrage* (undated), p. 6.

[2] *Chartist Circular*, Sept. 5, 1840, italics in the original.

Six million non-electors could sooner wrest their rights from 800,000 electors, than four millions could from three. Indeed, we should lose support, instead of gaining strength: now, great numbers of the middle class, being unenfranchised, are with us, because they want the vote—give them the vote, and having all they want—we can calculate on their support no longer.[1]

The Chartists not only refused to work with the Radicals for a partial extension of the franchise but regarded any other political reforms which were not accompanied by manhood suffrage as positive perils to democracy. The ballot was approved as one of the six points of the Charter; standing by itself, it was considered a menace, since it deprived the unenfranchised masses of the indirect influence they had been accustomed to exercise at election by cheering or groaning as the voters announced their choice. Besides intimidation at the polls, the workers had another and more potent means of control over elections, namely, the boycott of tradesmen who failed to please their customers by their votes. The aristocracy openly resorted to this form of coercion at every election, and Chartists were advised to follow the example thus set them.[2] The Chartists regarded the unrestrained power of an enfranchised minority to vote as it chose without reference to public opinion as comparable to secret balloting in Parliament.[3] As the *Chartist Circular* put the matter:

The franchise being limited, a power was vested by law in a given number of individuals, to perform a certain duty not for their own benefit—not according to their own pleasure, but for the good of the whole community,—would it then be reasonable to afford these men—men acting as agents for others,

[1] *Notes to the People*, p. 32.

[2] *Ibid.*, p. 225.

[3] *Bronterre's National Reformer*, Jan. 15, 1837.

to perform that duty secretly—to remove themselves completely from the control of those for whose interests they were, or at least ought to be, acting?[1]

The other points of the Charter were urged by the Chartists as much upon the basis of class interest as of democratic theory. The redistribution clauses of the Reform Bill of 1832 had only touched the more glaring anomalies of representation. According to a census taken on March 30, 1851, the represented boroughs of Tower Hamlets, Liverpool, Marylebone, Finsbury, Manchester (City), Lambeth, Westminster (City), and Birmingham, with a combined population of 2,651,915, sent only sixteen members to Parliament, while an equal representation was accorded to the boroughs of Wells (City), Evesham, Dartmouth, Harwich, Totnes, Thetford, Lyme Regis, Ashburton, Honiton, and Arundel, whose population totaled only 39,917.[2] Many important English boroughs were still without any special representation; among the metropolitan districts, Chelsea and Kensington, among the provincial towns, Birkenhead, Burnley, and Staleybridge, each with more than twenty thousand population. The inequalities in the counties were nearly as bad; the West Riding of Yorkshire sent two members to the House of Commons from a population of 794,779, while the population of Rutland, also returning two, was only 22,983. The distribution of seats in Parliament had a distinct class significance, since the boroughs and counties which were without adequate representation were the centers of large industrial populations, sure to be either Radical or Chartist in their sympathies. The necessity, then, for a redistribution of seats in accordance with population seemed as great, from

[1] *Chartist Circular*, Oct. 26, 1839.
[2] *Parliamentary Papers*, 1852 (441), xlii, 491 *et seq.*

the Chartist point of view, as the necessity for a widened suffrage.

The property qualification for membership in the House of Commons required for representatives of English and Welsh counties an annual income from landed property of six hundred pounds; members for boroughs, three hundred pounds.[1] This restriction did not apply to Scotland, nor to university representatives, and even in the English counties and boroughs it was often evaded or openly flouted. Nevertheless, this property qualification, taken in connection with the absence of any remuneration for members of Parliament, made it practically impossible for the Chartists to secure any representation without going outside their own class for their leaders, and this they were very reluctant to do. " Of what use," asked Lovett, " is the giving me the vote and freedom of choice if I can only choose rich men? "[2]   The ballot was advocated by the Chartists as a protection to the poor voter from coercion by landlord or employer; as we have seen [3] they cared nothing for the ballot unless accompanied by manhood suffrage. Annual elections for Parliament were deemed necessary to keep the people's representatives from losing touch with their constituents. The Chartists felt that each of the six points was not only just in itself but could hardly fail to strengthen the radical and weaken the conservative forces in British politics, always provided that their program was enacted as a unit.

The Chartists may have insisted too narrowly upon the

---

[1] By a law passed in 1838 (I and II Vict., c. 48), personal as well as real property qualified for membership.

[2] H. Solly, *James Woodford, Carpenter and Chartist*, 2 vols. (London, 1881). The citation is from a letter of William Lovett to the author, printed in the appendix of the book.

[3] *Cf. supra*, p. 24.

exact terms of their Charter, but they never fell into the
the error of treating political power as a sufficient goal for
their efforts.   The franchise they valued rather as an indispensable means for social and economic ends than for its
own sake.   Perhaps the most familiar illustration of this
point of view of the leaders of the movement is from the
speech of the Reverend J. R. Stephens, the Tory-Chartist,
at Kersal Moor, near Manchester:

The question of universal suffrage was, after all, a knife and
fork question.   If any man asked him what he meant by universal suffrage, he would tell him, he meant to say that every
working man in the land had a right to have a good coat and
hat, a good roof over his head, a good dinner upon his table,
no more work than would keep him in health, and as much
wages as would keep him in plenty, and the enjoyment of
those pleasures of life which a reasonable man could desire.[1]

Ernest Jones asked with equal emphasis: " What do we
want political power for, except to grant free access to all
the means of labour, land and machinery?"[2]   Friedrich
Engels claimed in 1844 that there was no longer a mere
politician among the Chartists.[3]   Of course Engels may
have been prejudiced by his desire to identify Chartism
with international Socialism, but it would be difficult to
bring any evidence against his statement.

Chartism was not only an economic movement, it was a
class movement.   The London Working Men's Association
of 1837, which would admit only laborers to its active
membership, printed on its membership card: " The man
who evades his share of useful labour diminishes the public

---

[1] *Annual Register*, vol. lxxx (1838), p. 311.

[2] *Notes to the People*, p. 301.

[3] F. Engels, *Condition of the Working Class in England in 1844*
(London, 1892; reprint from 1845), p. 235.

stock of wealth, and throws his own burden upon his neighbour ".[1] Manhood suffrage was in the eyes of many not a question of the enfranchisement of individuals but of a hitherto unrepresented class. One Chartist paper even declared that " a constituency equal to our present one . . . might serve the purposes of good government as well as one ten times as large, or as well as universal suffrage itself ", if it could only be arranged somehow that the new electorate should be " fairly selected from all classes of the community, in contingents proportional to their respective numbers ".[2] It is, then, as a class-conscious proletarian agitation, similar to modern Socialism in its spirit if not quite so definite in its program, that Chartism must always be considered.

The conservative opponents of Chartism were even more explicit about the economic aims of the movement than were its leaders. Their arguments were rarely directed against the abstract principle of manhood suffrage, but took, as a rule, one of two forms, that the Chartists were visionaries who held the erroneous idea that the mere possession of political power could alter the great unvarying laws of political economy in their favor, or that they were a party of revolutionists determined to use the six points as a means to effect the confiscation of all property. Lord John Russell, who took the former view of the agitation, wrote in 1839:

Of the working classes who have declared their adherence to what is called the People's Charter, but few care for Universal Suffrage, Vote by Ballot, or Annual Parliaments. The greater part feel the hardship of their social condition; they complain of their hard toil and insufficient wages, and imagine that Mr.

---

[1] R. G. Gammage, *History of the Chartist Movement*, p. 9.
[2] *Power of the Pence*, Feb. 10, 1849.

Oastler or Mr. Fielden will lead them to a happy valley, where
their labor will be light, and their wages high.[1]

Other conservatives, usually of the Tory type, saw a more
definite and sinister purpose in the movement. In the opinion of *Blackwood's Magazine,* " What is meant, under any
mystification of words we need not say, is—one universal
partition, amongst the nineteen millions in this island, of
the existing property, be its nature what it may, and under
whatsoever tenure ".[2] Two further citations from the
same periodical carry us further into the details of this
threatened general expropriation:

Within three weeks, were it merely to earn their wages, the
new house of legislators would have abolished all funded property, under the showy pretence of remitting to the people that
annual thirty millions of taxes requisite for meeting the interest. Their second step would be, what already they parade
as an " equitable distribution " of property.[3]

Repudiation of state engagements . . . confiscation of property under the name of a graded income tax; the abolition of
primogeniture, in order to ruin the landed interest; the issue
of assignats, in order to sustain the state under the shock to
credit which such measures would necessarily occasion, might
with confidence be looked for.[4]

William Lovett and John Collins, writing from War-
wick gaol, admitted that the two chief arguments of their
opponents had been the fear of the repudiation of the
national debt,[5] and the denial of property rights in gen-

---

[1] *Letter to the Electors of Stroud,* p. 33.

[2] *Blackwood's Magazine,* Sept., 1842.

[3] *Ibid.*

[4] *Ibid.,* June, 1848.

[5] *Chartism,* by Wm. Lovett and John Collins (London, 1841), p. 18.

eral,[1] and attempted to reassure their readers on these points. That they were right in believing that the real objection to their propaganda was fear of the economic consequences if it should succeed, is proved by the debate in the House of Commons upon the question of considering the Chartist petition of 1842.[2] Lord John Russell disclaimed any hostility to the principle of democracy as such, saying:

I can well believe, that in the United States of America—the only country which I should at all compare with this for the enjoyment of liberty and the full fruits of civilization—I can well believe, that in that country, where there is no monarchy, where every office is elective, where there is no established church, where there are not great masses of property, universal suffrage may be exercised without injury to order, and without danger to the general security of society.[3]

Thomas Babington Macaulay took a similar position, declaring that he would not oppose universal suffrage even for the sake of preserving the existence of the crown and of the House of Lords, for these institutions were after all but means to an end, adding, however: " I believe that universal suffrage would be fatal to all purposes for which government exists, and for which aristocracies and all other things exist, and that it is incompatible with the very existence of civilization.   I conceive that civilization rests on the security of property." [4]   Then he proceeded to paint a picture of the England of the future when property rights would no longer be safeguarded by a suffrage limited to men who had property of their own to protect:

---

[1] *Chartism, op. cit.*, p. 22.

[2] *Cf. infra*, p. 61.

[3] *Hansard*, 3d series, vol. lxiii, pp. 74-75.

[4] *Hansard, op. cit.*, p. 46.

I do not wish to say all that forces itself upon my mind with regard to what might be the result of our granting the Charter. . . . A great community of human beings—a vast people would be called into existence in a new position; there would be a depression, if not an utter stoppage, of trade, and of all those vast engagements of the country by which our people were supported, and how is it possible to doubt that famine and pestilence would come before long to wind up the effects of such a system. The best thing which I can expect, and which I think everyone must see as the result, is, that in some of the desperate struggles which must take place in such a state of things, some strong military despot must arise, and give some sort of protection—some security to the property which may remain.[1]

The conservative view of the Chartist movement no doubt exaggerated both the intentions of the leaders and their probable ability to carry their views into effect even in a House of Commons chosen on the basis of the six points, but it was right in supposing that the mainspring of the agitation was the desire of the working classes, especially in the great industrial towns, to improve their economic condition. To accomplish this, it is certainly true that the Chartist leaders without exception were in favor of legislation which would tend to secure " an equitable distribution of property ", although some sought this readjustment through the abolition of existing " class legislation ", while others proposed legislative programs more or less socialistic in character.

One of the chief abuses which the Chartists ascribed to the class character of the suffrage was the amount and kind of taxation to which the masses of the English people were subject. As the *Edinburgh Review* correctly stated the position of the Chartists, " On one point they would prob-

---

[1] *Hansard, op. cit.*, pp. 50-51.

ably all agree—one reform they have long been taught by their leaders to regard as the most important and unquestionable of all,—*viz.*, a reduction in the amount, and an alteration in the incidence, of taxation." [1] They objected particularly to the accumulation of the national debt. By 1842 the total debt, funded and unfunded, had increased by more than ten million pounds during the decade of the reformed parliamentary régime, reaching a total of £791,-757,816.[2] Interest and other annual charges had increased by that time to £29,300,112. In their " National Petition " of 1842 the Chartists spoke of the national debt in terms which caused more comment and alarm among the members of Parliament than any thing else in the petition:

Your petitioners complain that they are taxed to pay the interest of what is termed the National Debt—a debt amounting at present to eight hundred millions of pounds—being only a portion of the enormous amount expended in cruel and expensive wars for the suppression of all liberty, by men not authorized by the people, and who, consequently, had no right to tax posterity for the outrages committed by them upon mankind.[3]

It would be unfair to assume from the mere fact that the Chartists denounced the national debt that they were prepared to outlaw it without compensation; although conservative fears were in a measure excused by the fact that some of the party had expressed the hope that " the fundholder's title to draw interest " might one day be abolished.[4]

---

[1] *Edinburgh Review*, January, 1852.

[2] *Parliamentary Papers*, 1857-8 (443), xxxiii, 165 *et seq.*

[3] The whole text of the petition is given in *Hansard*, 3d series, vol. xlii, pp. 1376-81.

[4] *Chartist Circular*, March 7, 1840.

The Chartists were not at one as to the proper principles
of national finance; but they all favored direct as opposed to
indirect taxation and they all favored a use of the taxing
power, not only in such a way as to raise the needed revenue
and to equalize the burden of governmental expenditure,
but also to lessen the existing inequalities in the distribution
of wealth.   A Chartist periodical put this intention with
remarkable frankness: " In theory, a property tax is the
most equitable one that could be desired.   Its principles and
meaning are to mulct the rich for the poor, to level wealth,
and to produce social equilibrium." [1]   Ernest Jones, in-
cidentally asserting the Marxian doctrine of the inevitable
centralization of wealth, expressed the same view: " Wealth
[in America] is beginning to centralize.   It is in its nature
—all other evils follow in its wake.   It should be the duty of
government to counteract that centralization by laws having a distributive tendency." [2]   William Lovett, the acknowledged chief of the moderate or " moral force "
Chartists, also praised direct taxation and favored the absorption of the " unearned increment " of land values.[3]
J. Bronterre O'Brien, called by Feargus O'Connor " the
schoolmaster " of the Chartists, held that the land rental
" would form a national fund adequate to defray all charges
of the public service . . . without the necessity for any
taxation." [4]

J. Bronterre O'Brien and Ernest Jones were zealous champions of the principle of co-operation, and promised themselves that a Parliament reformed on the basis of the

[1] *Power of the Pence*, Dec. 23, 1848.

[2] *Notes to the People*, p. 2.

[3] Lovett, *Social and Political Morality* (London, 1853), p. 191.

[4] *Propositions of the National Reform League for the Peaceful Regeneration of Society* (1850).

Charter would subsidize co-operative industry. Their purpose should be: " To put an end to profitmongering—to emancipate the working-classes from wages-slavery, by enabling them to become their own masters; to destroy monopoly and to counteract the centralization of wealth, by its equable and general diffusion." [1] O'Brien proposed to establish the right of the people to " a share in the public credit of the state, in the form of temporary loans or advances from the proceeds of the rents, mines, fisheries, and other public property," in order that the people might " be able to stock and crop the lands rented from the State, or to manufacture on their own account." [2] Ernest Jones turns aside from a bitter attack upon the ineffectiveness of the attempts which had been made at co-operative production to ask: " But how would it be, if they had political power to give them a start? If they had a House of Commons to vote them £100,000,000 sterling, levied by direct taxation on the rich? " [3] He would, however, have nothing to do with any co-operative enterprises which were operated upon less than a national scale, believing that such would only become new centers of privilege.

Then what is the only salutary basis for co-operative industry? A *national* one. All co-operation should be founded, not on isolated efforts, absorbing, if successful, vast riches to themselves, but on a national union which should distribute the national wealth. To make these associations secure and beneficial, you must make it their interest to *assist* each other, instead of competing with each other—you must give them *unity of action*, and *identity of interest*. [4]

[1] *Notes to the People*, p. 27.

[2] *Labor's Wrongs and Labor's Remedy* (undated pamphlet), p. 4. Cf. *National Regeneration League, op. cit.*, p. 3.

[3] *Notes to the People*, p. 603.

[4] *Ibid.*, p. 30. The italics are in the original.

The land monopoly was one of the chief grievances of the Chartists, although it cannot be listed as one of the causes of the movement since the enclosure of the common lands was chiefly consummated about a generation earlier.[1] This may be illustrated by the successive decrease in the number of acts of enclosure passed in each of the preceding decades of the century.[2]

```
From 1800 to 1810 ................................. 905
From 1810 to 1820 ................................. 741
From 1820 to 1830 ................................. 192
From 1830 to 1840 ................................. 125
```

And yet the process of enclosure had by no means stopped. In 1841, twenty-two acts of enclosure were passed, and in 1842 twelve.[3] The total amount of land which passed to private owners by these means from 1760 to 1843 was probably nearly seven million acres.[4] Briefly, the economic changes of the eighteenth and the early nineteenth centuries transformed England from a country remarkable for the number of its independent peasantry, to one conspicuous by their comparative absence. The British freehold farmers have never recovered their former importance; and, as late as the great land survey of 1874-1875, the total number of independent holdings in England and Wales, exclusive of wastes, common, house and garden plots of less than an acre, was only 269,547, and half of the agricultural land of the country was owned by a few more than two thousand persons.[5]

[1] For the beginnings of the enclosure movement, E. C. K. Gonner, *Common Land and Inclosure* (London, 1912).

[2] *Parliamentary Papers*, 1843 (325), xlviii, 467.   [3] *Ibid.*

[4] A. Toynbee, *Lectures on the Industrial Revolution* (London, 1884), p. 89.

[5] *Report of the Land Enquiry Committee* (London, 1913), vol. i, introd. by Gilbert Slater, p. 83.

It is true that Chartism was essentially an urban movement and drew its strength in overwhelming preponderance from the industrial towns of Lancashire and the other northern counties. But it had no such opposition to the " agricultural interest " as was shown by the manufacturers and their representatives in Parliament. On the contrary, the Chartists were among the strongest opponents of the new industrial system and earnestly desired to get a large proportion of the factory workers back to the land. It was chiefly by taking advantage of the strength of this feeling that Feargus O'Connor was able to commit the entire movement to the success of his land plan.[1] But while the Chartists saw a common grievance in British landlordism they were by no means agreed among themselves as to the appropriate remedy. Some favored the nationalization of the land; others wished to establish a peasant proprietorship. The sharp divergence between these factions effectively prevented any union of the party upon a land program. It would not, however, be going too far to say that, however the Chartist leaders might differ upon the question of land ownership, they were agreed that the land must be restored to the people, that the great estates must be broken up into small farms, and that the principle of primogeniture in the entailing of land must be abolished.

The attack on the land monopoly was not regarded as a novel attack on property, but simply as a restitution of rights once enjoyed and now unjustly withheld. The Chartist periodicals ever kept before the mind of their readers the idea that until the Tudor period almost all of the land of England was held by the yeomanry, and that this had been stolen from them bit by bit ever since through the class legislation which was the inevitable result of the restriction

[1] *Cf. infra,* pp. 84-93.

of the franchise.   All of the acts of enclosure were regarded
as part of this program of theft.   In speaking of the land
monopoly in Scotland, Ernest Jones concluded his attack:
" Behold evil and remedy.   Down with the 7800 landed
monopolists.   Restore the wages-slaves to those lands of
which their forefathers were plundered.   And behold the
means in political power and in that alone." [1]   The right of
access to the land was regarded not only as an historic right,
but as a natural right as well.   " Every man who is willing
to cultivate land and render it productive . . . should be
allowed to possess a portion of land. . . . No man should
be allowed to keep land in his possession uncultivated." [2]

Since the Chartists were convinced that the right to ex-
propriate the landlord was so clear, the only remaining question was the wisdom of this policy.   Many economists of
the day believed not only that the small farm was doomed
to disappear in competition with the estate of the capitalist,
but that this change, so far from being reactionary, was the
way of progress.   The enclosure movement had undeniably
been accompanied by much agricultural improvement.   The
" gentleman farmer " invested heavily in the new machinery,
tried experiments in stock-breeding, and spent a great deal
in manuring and draining the soil.   The theories of Arthur
Young, advocate of the " new farming," dominated British
economic thought.   Chartism, in fact, was at its strongest
just when this contrast between the new farming and the
old was most marked, for the chief improvements of modern
farming were then both known and used, but the average
farmer had neither the capital nor the education to enable
him to make use of them for himself.   But the Chartists, in
defiance of the regnant ideas of the time, championed the
small farm system.   They acknowledged that the weight of

---

[1] *Notes to the People*, p. 444.

[2] *The Reformer's Almanac*, by Joseph Barker (London, 1848), p. 17.

contemporary authority was against them, but set down all opposition as due to the prejudices of the privileged. " There is amongst some," wrote Joseph Barker, " an outcry against small farms; but we believe the outcry originates with selfish men." [1]   Ernest Jones estimated that an equal division of the arable land in the United Kingdom would give eleven acres to every family.[2]

The chief cause of the opposition to the institution of primogeniture seems to have been that it was an artificial means of maintaining the system of great estates which the Chartists believed to be so radically vicious. The question was brought forcibly to the attention of the nation in the formative year of the movement. Mr. Ewart had introduced a bill into the House of Commons on the fourth of April, 1837, making real property subject to the same laws of entail as other private property. It was rejected by a majority of thirty-three.[3] The smallness of the vote, twenty-one to fifty-four, shows how far outside the field of practical politics such a measure then was. The Chartists, however, were willing to go even beyond the scope of the measure rejected by Parliament and to favor legislation which would compel the division of landed property at death. William Lovett insisted that the testator " should not be empowered to determine that his property should pass on successively from heir to heir, to the prejudice of the younger branches of the family." [4]   Joseph Barker held it was the law of entail and primogeniture that gave to the aristocracy their power, and added that, compared with this one evil, all other political evils were as nothing.[5]

[1] *Reformer's Companion to the Almanac* (Wortley, 1848), p. 153.
[2] *Notes to the People*, p. 111.
[3] *Hansard*, 3d series, vol. xxxvii, p. 740.
[4] *Social and Political Morality*, p. 165.
[5] *Companion to the Almanac, op. cit.*, p. 123.

But the agreement of the Chartist leaders as to the economic purposes for which they valued the franchise was wholly negative. All were opposed to a system of taxation which bore more hardly upon the poor than upon the rich, to the further accumulation of the public debt, to the land monopoly and to the principle of primogeniture. But there was no corresponding positive economic program. Some Chartists favored free-trade; others were protectionist. Some believed in peasant proprietorship and in voluntary co-operation; others desired the nationalization of the land and state ownership of industry. Some wished to work hand in glove with the labor unions, the co-operative stores and the Owenite Socialists; others dreaded the effect of an alliance between the Chartist party and any parallel or competing reform movement. Disregarding minor points of difference, we may distinguish three main factions within the party on the question of property in the means of production and of distribution.

Ernest Jones was the intellectual leader of the extreme collectivists of the party. Their aims were best phrased in the resolutions adopted by the Chartist convention of 1851, at a time when the organized movement was completely in the hands of this faction. These resolutions favored the complete nationalization of the land by government resumption of commons, crown lands and the lands of the Church, and by purchase from private owners; the disestablishment and disendowment of the Church of England; free, compulsory, secular education; the founding of national co-operative societies; the establishment of the right of the poor to relief and employment; the placing of all taxes on land or on property; the extinction of the national debt by treating interest payments as installments of the principal; the substitution of a militia for a standing army, and the abolition of capital punishment.[1]

[1] *The Friend of the People*, April 12, 1851.

As we have already seen, Ernest Jones was at once the strongest advocate of co-operation on a national scale and the bitterest opponent of the co-operative movement of the time.[1] He viewed with equal suspicion the attempt to create a peasant proprietorship by increasing the number of small holdings, fearing lest a numerous body of small owners would prove a bulwark for the protection of large landowners as well, since both would have an interest in upholding the principle of private property in land.[2] " There is nothing," he wrote, " more *reactionary* than the small freehold system. It is increasing the strength of landlordism." [3]   In common with other Chartists, he held that the small farm system was far superior to the English capitalistic agriculture, but he regarded this as only a relative superiority. Better results than were obtainable by either of the existing methods might be obtained if the land were nationalized.[4] With that accomplished, " such a thing as pauperism, in its real sense, could hardly exist." [5] It is surprising, in view of his opinions, that Jones worked for years as the closest ally of Feargus O'Connor whose pet plan was to establish just such a class of freehold farmers as Jones had denounced.

Two of the most important and influential of the Chartist leaders, opposed on almost every point of policy, led the

[1] *Supra,* p. 34.

[2] It is worth notice that Charles Kingsley opposed O'Connor's land plan on the ground that peasant proprietorship was a reactionary system, tending to sink the peasant into an animal and slavish condition. " For the town artizan . . . to become a peasant proprietor would be, I conceive, nothing but a fall." *The Application of Associative Principles and Methods to Agriculture* (1851), p. 59.

[3] *Notes to the People,* p. 56. Italics are in the original.

[4] *Ibid.,* pp. 256-7.

[5] *Ibid.,* p. 120.

individualist wing of the party. Feargus O'Connor wrote in *The Labourer,* a periodical which he edited in conjunction with Ernest Jones in the interests of his land plan:

I ever have been, and I think I ever shall be, opposed to the principle of Communism, as advocated by several theorists. I am, nevertheless, a strong advocate of Co-operation, which means legitimate exchange, and which circumstances would compel individuals to adopt, to the extent that Communism would be beneficial.[1]

" I am," he reassured the public, " even opposed to public kitchens, public baking-houses, and public wash-houses." [2] William Lovett was quite as outspoken. He thought that land nationalization, or even ownership vested in the municipalities or other local bodies, would be not only unnecessary but positively harmful. " Were the land divided into districts," he predicted, " and cultivated in common, and governed by majorities (locally or generally), there is reason for believing that the energies and virtues of the industrious, skilful, and saving, would soon be sunk and sacrificed for the benefit of the idle and extravagant." [3]

Lovett's own inclination was always for social improvement through voluntary effort, without waiting for the day when the Charter should become law and the action of the state on behalf of the people become possible. In the little booklet *Chartism,*[4] he advocated the establishment of a National Association to be supported by penny-a-week contributions which should maintain places for public meeting, schools, circulating libraries, public baths, play grounds,

[1] *The Labourer* (1847-8), p. 149.
[2] *Ibid.,* p. 157.
[3] *Social and Political Morality,* p. 163.
[4] *Cf. supra,* p. 29.

and the like. This preoccupation with popular education and general welfare was viewed with no little suspicion by some of Lovett's fellow Chartists, who feared lest the attention of reformers might be diverted from the all-important matter of winning the Charter.

Perhaps a third school of economic theory might be distinguished within the movement. J. Bronterre O'Brien cannot be wholly identified with the individualism of Lovett and O'Connor nor with the collectivism of Ernest Jones. He favored the nationalization of the land on the ground that " the nation alone has the just power of leasing out the land for cultivation and of appropriating the rents therefrom ".[1] To this end he advocated purchase by the government of all private land upon the death of the owner of each holding and its subsequent division into small farms paying rent to the state.[2] And yet he opposed communism in anything *but* land. O'Brien's cautious statement that " if the means of acquiring and retaining wealth are equally secured to all in proportion to the respective industry and services of each, I see no objection to private property ",[3] might seem to impose a rather stringent condition upon the institution of private property were it not for his optimistic conclusion that this just distribution of private wealth was by no means an impossibility. " I will never admit," he continues, " that private property is incompatible with public happiness, till I see it fairly tried. I never found an objection urged against it, which I cannot trace to the *abuse,* not to the *use,* of the institution." [4]

The explanation of O'Brien's position is the very sharp

---

[1] *Bronterre's National Reformer*, Feb. 25, 1837.

[2] *Labor's Wrongs and Labor's Remedy*, p. 4.

[3] *English Chartist Circular* (1841-2), vol. i, p. 71.

[4] Italics in the original.

distinction he drew between land and other forms of wealth. Land, minerals, and other forms of natural wealth ought to be nationalized, " because these are of God's and not man's creation ",[1] but we are not to fall into the " fatal delusion " of communism in the products of industry. Joseph Barker, another Chartist journalist of ability and influence, held that taxation should rest only on land, since " the land is not the produce of industry, but is itself wealth, independent of industry ".[2] Barker did not, however, draw the conclusion from this principle that the land should be nationalized or even that all its rental value should be absorbed by the state. In his view the state should impose only such a land tax as might be necessary to meet the current expenses of government. In the doctrines of O'Brien and Barker it is easy to see foreshadowings of Henry George and the theory of the Single Tax.

But however Chartists might differ as to the ultimate aims which the Charter was to make possible, all were agreed that political power was a certain means to achieve the aims which each of them desired. It did not apparently occur to any Chartist leader that a democratic House of Commons could fail to enact all necessary reforms, although the divisions of opinion within the Chartist party itself should have warned the Chartists of possible disappointment. Neither did they believe it possible that an unreformed Parliament would ever enact any but class legislation. " A parliament," insisted O'Brien, " which represents only those who thrive by labour's wrongs will never recognize labor's rights, nor legislate for labor's emancipation ".[3] He did not believe that any considerable num-

---

[1] *Power of the Pence*, Jan. 27, 1849.

[2] *The People* (1849), vol. i, p. 115.

[3] O'Brien, *The Rise, Progress and Phases of Human Slavery* (London, 1885; first edition in 1850), p. 119.

ber of the working class could hope to acquire property enough by their own efforts to entitle them to citizenship. " Knaves will tell you that it is because you have no property that you are unrepresented. I tell you, on the contrary, it is because you are unrepresented that you have no property ".[1] S. B. Bamford summed up the party attitude admirably: " Quoting scripture, we did, in fact say, first obtain annual parliaments, and universal suffrage, and, ' Whatsoever thou wouldest shall be added thereto '." [2] The Chartist movement resembled all modern proletarian movements in that its aims were economic, but it differed from more recent agitations by a unique belief in the efficacy of political action as a means.

But the aims and theories of Chartist leaders do not suffice to determine the character of the movement. Not only had all six points of the Charter been familiar to English radicals for decades, but all of the economic and social changes advocated or discussed in the Chartist press found champions before Chartism was organized and ever since it disappeared. The real question of the growth and decline of Chartism is the question of the varying amount of popular support afforded to the organization and its leaders. Chartism gave the British operative a standard to which to rally; it was to him what Socialism is to-day, the political party which seemed most adequately to express his grievances and to offer the most plausible remedy for them. The recruits of the Chartist movement were drawn from the supporters of a number of previous popular agitations. The chief of these have been summarized by Dr. Tildsley as follows:

[1] *Bronterre's National Reformer*, Jan. 15, 1837.
[2] S. B. Bamford, *Passages in the Life of a Radical* (London, 1844), vol. i, p. 11.

The first of these movements was Owenism, the second the movement for the attainment of the Ten Hour Bill, the third sought the repeal of the New Poor Law, and the fourth . . . desired the defeat of Peel's Currency Bill of 1819 and expressed itself in favor of the expansion of the circulating medium. We can hardly add to these four movements as a fifth that which aimed at the repeal of the Corn Laws, for in 1837 such a movement was not yet organized. But from that time forth . . . there were few great workers' meetings in which these laws were not openly attacked. Their opponents increased and strengthened the Chartist movement.[1]

One factor in the influence of Chartism among the unrepresented classes was the lack of other adequate outlet for their discontent. While the suffrage remained restricted they could have no share, other than agitation, in the political life of the country, and labor was not at that time sufficiently organized to make possible an effective struggle with capital in the economic field. The early years of Chartism were a period of great weakness among the labor unions. In 1841 the organization of the English and Scottish stonemasons collapsed, the Lancashire textile workers' organizations were inactive, the ironfounders, the boilermakers, and the journeymen of the millwrights and steam-engine makers were unable to maintain their unions in the face of widespread unemployment. The Glasgow workers had been particularly demoralized by the prosecutions directed against their violent methods in 1839.[2] Chartism profited by this discouragement of the workers with their efforts to win better conditions for themselves without a preliminary attainment of political power. The greater number of trades-unionists declared for the Charter, al-

[1] *Die Entstehung der Chartistenbewegung*, pp. 10-11.

[2] Sidney and Beatrice Webb, *History of Trade Unionism* (London, 1911), p. 157.

though the trades unions never joined the movement in a body *as unions*.[1]

But the strongest recruiting agent for the movement was what Thomas Carlyle named " the condition of England question ".[2] Not only was the absolute degree of poverty great, but the sharp contrast existing between the misery and dependence of the masses and the opulence of the few edged discontent with bitterness. A very naïve confession of the extent of this inequality was made by the ultra-conservative *Blackwood's Magazine* in an article directed against any extension of the franchise.[3] " Out of nineteen million heads in this island ", so ran the estimate, " not three hundred thousand are connected with property sufficient to ensure the conservative instincts and sympathies of properties." The Chartist attitude towards the inequalities which *Blackwood's* recorded so complacently, is well shown in the bitter language of the petition of 1842:

That your petitioners, with all due respect and loyalty, would compare the daily income of the Sovereign Majesty with that of thousands of the working men of this nation; and whilst your petitioners have learned that her Majesty receives daily for her private use the sum of £164 17s. 10d., they have also ascertained that many thousands of the families of the labourers are only in the receipt of 3¾d. per head per day.[4]

It is hardly surprising that the Chartist agitation, with its definite and attractive political program and its indefinite, but equally attractive, promise of social and economic betterment, became the center of one of the most formidable popu-

---

[1] Sidney and Beatrice Webb, *op. cit.*, p. 158.

[2] T. Carlyle, *Chartism* (London, 1839), *passim*.

[3] *Blackwood's Magazine*, Sept., 1842.

[4] *Hansard*, 3d series, vol. lxxii, p. 1378.

lar movements in English history. It is more remarkable
that the British workingmen who took part in the movement
should have fought for the Charter without any considerable
body of allies from other ranks of society. The Radicals
had been the party of the people and they were, as a group,
sympathetic with the Chartist demand for complete political
democracy.[1] But the Chartists not only refused to consider
themselves as a wing of the Radical party, they regarded the
middle-class Radicals as their most inveterate enemies and
lost no opportunity to criticize their activities in the House
of Commons and to oppose their candidates at elections.
Much of this opposition was due no doubt to mere class
prejudice, a feeling that it was impossible for the operatives to work in the same party with their employers. But
the specific issues which brought the Chartists into antagonism with Radicals as well as with the Whig ministry, were
three in number: the Poor Law Amendment Act of 1834;
the negative attitude of the Radicals, as a party, to social
politics in general and to factory legislation in particular;
and the anti-Corn-Law agitation, which competed for popular favor with the six points of the Charter during the years
of greatest strength of the Chartist propaganda.

The attitude of the Chartists toward the activities of the
Anti-Corn-Law League is one that requires some explanation, since the demand for cheaper food was made on behalf
of the industrial workers in the towns, the very class that
formed the bulk of the Chartist party. Gammage believed
that the Chartists who opposed the League might be divided
into three groups: the masses who simply distrusted their
employers and all the legislation favored by them; Chartists,
like William Lovett, who favored free-trade but wished to
obtain the Charter first; and the faction of Feargus O'Connor

[1] *Cf. supra*, p. 18.

and J. Bronterre O'Brien, who feared that free-trade meant lower wages and greater power for the manufacturers.[1] Lovett and Hetherington, in a letter to the *Northern Star* of September 22, 1838, pointed out that the Charter would without doubt be followed by an immediate abrogation of the Corn Laws.[2]   John Mason, speaking at Leicester in 1840, charged the League with bad faith to the working classes, saying: " When we get the Charter we will repeal the Corn Laws and all the other bad laws.   But if you give up your agitation for the Charter to help the Free Traders, they will not help you to get the Charter . . . ' Cheap Bread! ' they cry.   But they mean low wages." [3]   The second resolution of the executive committee in 1842 declared :

That this meeting unreservedly condemns all taxes levied upon bread and other necessaries of life, that it is of the opinion that the monopoly of food depends upon the monopoly of the Suffrage, that it has no confidence in any Government appointed under the present system, and despairing of the removal of existing misery, is fully convinced that the total and entire repeal of the Corn and Provision Laws, can only be the act of a Parliament representing the interests and opinions of the whole people of Great Britain and Ireland.[4]

Henry Vincent also held the view expressed in this resolution that it would be easier as well as better to obtain the repeal of the Corn Laws through the medium of a Chartist House of Commons than to agitate for it directly.   Speaking at Bath on December 20, 1841, he gave as his opinion that nothing short of an agitation " almost bordering on

[1] Gammage, *op. cit.*, pp. 102-4.
[2] Cited in E. Dolléans, *Le Chartisme*, vol. ii, p. 24.
[3] *Life of Thomas Cooper*, p. 136.
[4] *English Chartist Circular*, vol. ii, p. 25.

a Revolution " could obtain a repeal of the Corn Laws, and that " the same amount of exertion would obtain a perfect control over the Government." [1]   The free-trade Chartists, then, regarded the activities of the Anti-Corn Law League as a harmful, perhaps deliberately harmful, division of the forces of reform which should be united upon the conquest of political democracy as a prerequisite to all economic reforms.

Other Chartists, however, cannot be classified as free-traders.   Many believed with the Ricardian economists that the amount of wages or the price of bread was a question of little permanent importance, since wages would tend in the long run to fall to mere subsistence.[2]   At a meeting in Manchester on March 19, 1841, the walls were covered with placards reading: " Why do these liberal manufac-turers bawl so lustily for the repeal of the Corn Laws? Because, with the reduced price of corn, they will be enabled to reduce the wages of the working men, in order that they may compete with foreigners who live upon potatoes." [3] Debates between the Chartists and the League were of fre quent occurrence and not seldom ended in riot and disorder.[4] With the repeal of the Corn Laws the attitude of many Chartists changed.   Previously the majority of the party promised themselves free-trade, at least in foodstuffs, as one of the results of the winning of the Charter.   Even those who cared nothing for free-trade did not adopt a protectionist theory, but contented themselves with the argu-ment that the Anti-Corn Law League sought the benefit of

---

[1] *English Chartist Circular*, vol. i, p. 201.

[2] Tildsley, *Die Entstehung der Chartistenbewegung*, p. 84.

[3] Archibald Prentice, *History of the Anti-Corn Law League*, 2 vols. (London, 1853), vol. i, pp. 192-3.

[4] *Cf. infra*, p. 157.

the manufacturers rather than that of the operatives. But after the victory of the League the Chartists could no longer contend that only a Chartist Parliament would repeal the Corn Laws, and it would weaken their propaganda to admit that an economic reform which was carried by an unrepresentative Parliament had been of great benefit to the working people. In 1841 an influential party periodical declared that the policy of the Chartists was " not to reduce, but to abolish the taxes on all articles which press upon the industry of the laborer, and give cheap tea, tobacco, coffee, wines, etc., at the same time with cheap bread, wood, and sugar." [1] In 1848 another Chartist paper insisted that, while direct taxation was the simpler and so the better method, yet the worker in the end paid all taxes and could gain little or nothing by abolishing the taxes which pressed on industry; " as to the ' taxes on industry,' as they are called, a repeal of them never benefits the laborer, but always the capitalist that employs him, or the fixed income man, who consumes his produce." [2]   " Free-trade," said this paper, " without reciprocity, without a reduction of rents and taxes, and without any guarantees to the working classes, against non-employment and reductions in wages, *was* and *is* a positive evil." [3]

The powerful influence of O'Connor was thrown against free trade. He hated the Whigs and the manufacturers so bitterly that he was almost willing to champion the " agricultural interest " against them. This position was especially marked when he became interested in his land plan for re-establishing a British peasantry. Naturally O'Connor feared the effect of foreign competition upon his agri-

---

[1] *McDouall's Chartist and Republican Journal*, May 29, 1841.

[2] *Power of the Pence*, Nov. 11, 1848.

[3] *Ibid.*, Jan. 20, 1849; italics in the original.

cultural venture, and he desired protection just as did other English landowners. Like other Chartists, too, he seems to have held the " home market " theory; considering that the working classes of Great Britain should be the best customers of the manufacturers of the nation, and viewing with suspicion the uncertainties of foreign trade.[1] Finally, it was remembered by all Chartists that John Bright and Richard Cobden, the most prominent representatives of free trade theory to the country at large, were at the same time the strongest opponents of factory legislation in the House of Commons.

The question of governmental regulation of the hours and conditions of labor brought the Chartists into sharpest conflict with the Radicals. The Radicals favored free trade as a commercial policy and unrestricted rights of contract[2] in industry. The Chartists did not share the Radical faith in the philosophy of *laissez-faire;* they were not agreed as to the benefits of free trade but they were unanimous in upholding the right of the state to supervise industry for the protection of labor. Harriet Martineau, writing as a Radical, thus scornfully characterized the Chartist position: " The Chartists understood nothing of the operation of the corn-laws against their interests; and they were so far from comprehending their own existing rights, while demanding others, that they permitted friends to urge the legislature to take from them the command of their only possession—their labor." [3] Miss Martineau was

[1] Tildsley, *op. cit.,* p. 89.

[2] Many of the Radicals drew a distinction between the labor of adults and that of children and did not oppose state interference to protect the latter, but even in child-labor legislation they were apt to be very conservative.

[3] H. Martineau, *A History of the Thirty Years' Peace,* 4 vols. (London, 1877), vol. iii, p. 494.

wholly correct in believing that the Chartists favored labor legislation to protect adults as well as children. This is proved by the language of their petition of 1842:

Your petitioners complain that the hours of labour, particularly of the Factory Workers, are protracted beyond the limits of human endurance, and that the wages earned, after unnatural application to toil in heated and unhealthy workshops, are inadequate to sustain the bodily strength, and supply those comforts which are so imperative after an excessive waste of physical energy.[1]

A few enlightened Tories such as Lord Ashley (later Earl of Shaftesbury) and a few such Radicals as John Fielden, were in full sympathy with the special interests of the working class. But the general position of Parliament during the earlier years of Chartist agitation was one of obstinate opposition to any such state interference with industry as the Chartists desired. As leader of the Conservatives, Sir Robert Peel opposed the attempt to limit the hours of labor for women and children employed in the textile factories to ten hours a day,[2] although it is true that he could not carry all of his party with him. John Bright, perhaps the greatest Radical leader, characterized the Ten Hours bill as " one of the worst measures ever passed in the shape of an act of the legislature ".[3] John Roebuck, another influential Radical, offered a resolution in 1844: " That it is the opinion of this House that no interference with the power of adult labourers in factories, to make contracts respecting the hours for which they shall be employed, be sanctioned by this House ".[4] Still more extreme expres-

---

[1] *Hansard*, 3d series, vol. lxii, pp. 1376-81.

[2] *Ibid.*, vol. lxxiv, pp. 1078-94.

[3] *Ibid.*, vol. lxxxix, p. 1148.

[4] *Ibid.*, vol. lxxiv, p. 611.

sions of the same attitude might be quoted. E. C. Tufnell enlivened his official report on factory conditions with the highly ingenuous remark that " the precise form of evil which the Ten Hour Bill would assume it is impossible to foresee, but certain it is, that nothing but evil could come from its operation ".[1] The Marquis of Londonderry, who had much property in coal mines, declared in the House of Lords that he would never allow his property to be inspected. " As a coal owner, he should say to any inspector, ' You may go down into the pit how you can, and when you are down, you may remain there '." [2]

Although the Chartists, unlike most of the other factory reformers, made no distinction between legislation for children and for adults, for women and for men, they supported every attempt made in Parliament to limit the labor of women and children. Besides the motives of humanity and the fact that the abuses of the existing industrial system appeared most clearly in the case of women and children, the British workingman had a double reason for favoring the proposed protective legislation. The cheapness of child labor and the simplicity of factory machinery endangered the workingman's own job, or at least his previous standard of wages, by forcing him to compete with his own children in the labor market.[3] In the second place, as the opponents of state regulation never wearied of pointing out, women, children and young persons were commonly employed as " helpers " or auxiliaries to the men who worked in the same establishment. A limitation of their labor operated in practise as a limitation of the labor of the men as well, and it was this limitation that the Radi-

[1] *Parliamentary Papers*, 1834, pt. i (167), xix, 259 *et seq.; * p. 214.

[2] *Hansard*, 3d series, vol. lxv, p. 891.

[3] On this point see *Parliamentary Papers*, 1833 (450), xx, 1 *et seq.,* 25.

cals were chiefly concerned to oppose and the Chartists to defend.

The other great issue between Radicals and Chartists was the Poor Law Amendment Act of 1834,[1] superseding the Elizabethan law of 1601 [2] and much subsequent legislation. J. H. Rose is of the opinion that in all probability " the People's Charter would never have been drawn up, but for the blaze of discontent caused by the exorbitant stamp duty on newspapers and by the severity of the new Poor Law of 1834 ",[3] and there is much contemporary evidence to confirm his view. Lord Stanhope declared in 1839 that " He saw, alas! too much reason to expect that, at a future and no distant period, a Radical Reformer— perhaps some Chartist—would exclaim, with joy and exultation . . . ' Without the new Poor Law we should never have had universal suffrage '." [4] The purpose of the new law was to decrease the burden of the poor rates which threatened, under the old sytem of parochial relief, to pauperize a large part of the English laborers, especially in the country; the method chosen to effect this was the practical abolition of outdoor relief and the consolidation of parishes into " unions " for purposes of administration.[5] Three commissioners were appointed to oversee the operation of the act throughout England and Wales generally, to make yearly reports of the working of the new system, to appoint minor officials, to issue instructions for the guidance of the local poor law authorities, and to order unions formed and workhouses built. Each parish in the union

[1] 4 and 5 William IV, c. 76.

[2] 43 Eliz., c. 2.

[3] Rose, *The Rise of Democracy* (London, 1897), p. 54.

[4] *Hansard*, 3d series, vol. xlviii, p. 806.

[5] The New Poor Law is described in G. Nicholls, *History of the English Poor Law*, 2 vols. (London, 1898), vol. ii, pp. 272-81.

was liable for the support of its own poor, but aid was extended through the medium of the union. Migration of labor was encouraged, in place of the penalization of the old Law of Settlement devised to prevent parishes from shifting their burdens onto each other. Two justices were allowed to except persons unable to work from the requirement of residence in the workhouse imposed upon other paupers. The regulations issued by the new commissioners to the boards of guardians forbade relief to all persons in employment, relief in money allowance to able-bodied workers, payments of house rent and outdoor relief generally, except in cases of urgent necessity, to persons from sixteen to sixty.[1] Within the unions paupers were separated into seven classes: aged or infirm men, men and youths over thirteen, boys from seven to thirteen, aged and infirm women, women and girls over sixteen, girls from seven to sixteen, and children under seven.[2] Even relatives were separated under this plan and allowed to meet only under restrictions. Paupers could not leave the workhouse even to go to church without going through all the formalities of readmission on their return.[3]

The success of the New Poor Law from the standpoint of its authors was great and immediate. In the year ending Lady-day, 1834, the last year before the change of system took place, £6,317,255 was spent for the relief of the poor, an amount equal to 8s. 9½d. per capita of the population of England and Wales.[4] The next year the sum had fallen to £5,526,418, or 7s. 7d. per capita; while in 1836-37 it was only £4,044,741, or 5s. 5d. per capita. Afterwards the hard times increased the cost of poor relief

---

[1] Nicholls, *op. cit.*, p. 298.   [2] *Ibid.*, p. 301.

[3] Nicholls, *History of the English Poor Law, op. cit.*, pp. 311-2.

[4] Parliamentary Papers, 1852 (1461), xxiii, 1 *et seq.*

somewhat, but never quite to the old level throughout the entire period of Chartist agitation. Such stringent limitation of public charity, however, could not but attract criticism from many quarters. It was charged in Parliament in 1838 that Assistant Commissioner Kaye had declared that the intention of the authorities was " to make the workhouses as like prisons as possible, and to make them as uncomfortable as possible ", in order to terrorize British workingmen from seeking relief.[1] Fortunately for the popular acceptance of the law it was passed during a period of industrial expansion which permitted rural laborers to find work in the industrial towns of the midland and the north.[2] But, nevertheless, the first effect of the change was to force many of the aged or infirm agricultural laborers into the workhouses of the unions,[3] and also, apparently, to increase the labor of women and children in the rural districts.[4] With the coming of hard times in 1837 the workmen in the towns felt the rigor of the new system, and, both in town and in country, meetings of protest were held. Richard Oastler, of Yorkshire, and in Lancashire the Reverend Joseph Raynor Stephens, a Wesleyan minister, counseled resistance to the enforcement of the law. At Newcastle, on New Year's Day, 1838, Stephens told his hearers that rather than have the law continued he would prefer to see Newcastle " one blaze of fire with only one way to put it out, and that with the blood of all who supported this abominable measure ".[5]

The Chartists found powerful allies outside their own

[1] *Hansard*, 3d series, vol. xli, p. 1014.

[2] W. Hasbach, *History of the English Agricultural Labourer* (London, 1908), p. 220.

[3] *Ibid.*, p. 219.

[4] *Ibid.*, p. 225.

[5] Gammage, *History of the Chartist Movement*, pp. 55-9.

ranks in their struggle with the New Poor Law. The adherents of factory reform, including the Tory Democrats and the London *Times*, protested against the severity of the law; partly, no doubt, from a genuine sympathy with the poor, but partly because it was carried by a Whig ministry and a reformed Parliament. No one could forget the exclamation of William Cobbett at the friendly reception accorded to the hated measure by the House of Commons, " Thank God! The country still possessed a House of Lords; and while that tribunal existed the poor man had no reason to despair of justice." [1] The Poor Law Amendment Act passed the House of Lords without much difficulty, but Cobbett's words were partly justified by a formal protest printed by some of the Lords declaring the measure " unjust and cruel to the poor ".[2] The members of the reformed Parliament, such as Attwood and O'Connor, who afterwards sympathized with Chartism, joined with Cobbett to oppose the Bill in all its stages. Attwood, at a later period, declared the New Poor Law " more odious than any measure which had been passed since the Norman Conquest." [3] But the leaders of both the Liberal and the Conservative parties steadily opposed all attempts to reopen the questions which it was hoped that the law of 1834 had settled.

To the Chartists, the New Poor Law was not only a grievance but a breach of faith. They had come to look upon the outdoor relief granted for so many generations not as a charity to be extended or withdrawn at the whim of a legislature in which they had no representation, but as one of the historic *rights* of the English laborer. Cobbett

---

[1] *Hansard*, 3d series, vol. xxiv, p. 387.

[2] *Ibid.*, vol. xxv, p. 1098.

[3] *Ibid.*, vol. xlix, p. 223.

had declared that everyone ought to know " that the right of the English poor to relief in cases of indigence was as sound and as good a right as that of any gentleman or nobleman to the possession of his lands." [1] This exactly corresponded with the view expressed seven years later by one of the Chartists:

I would undertake to prove that the poor had a better right to such parochial relief as the old Act of Elizabeth provided, than the landlord has to his conquered estate or the grinding shopocrat to his fraud-begotten profits. . . I would go further and prove that the legislature had no more right (except the right of force) to pass such an act as the amendment act (without giving the paupers and labouring classes compensation) than it had to rifle the silversmiths of London of their plate to make coin of it.[2]

The workers suspected in the policy of the government a capitalist plot to drive them to accept cheap labor by cutting off their old alternative of poor relief.[3] They also criticized the meager dietary of the union workhouses, comparing the pauper allowance with the payments to " national out-door paupers " such as the royal family;[4] and they denounced the segregation of husbands and wives as a violation of the law of God. The emphatic attitude of the Chartists on the question of poor relief is well illustrated by their petition of 1842, in which they take occasion to denounce as " contrary to all previous statutes, opposed to the spirit of the constitution, and an actual violation of the Christian religion "

---

[1] *Hansard*, 3d series, vol. xxiii, p. 1336.

[2] *McDouall's Chartist and Republican Journal*, Aug. 21, 1841.

[3] Tildsley, *Die Entstehung der Chartistenbewegung*, p. 27.

[4] *The New Black List*, cited in Dierlamm, *Die Flugschriftenliteratur der Chartistenbewegung*, p. 23.

the determination of your honourable House to continue the Poor-law Bill in operation, notwithstanding the many proofs which have been afforded by sad experience of the unconstitutional principle of the bill, of its unchristian character, and of the cruel and murderous effects produced upon the wages of working men, and the lives of the subjects of this realm.[1]

The Chartist movement, if it did not take name and form until three or four years after the Poor Law Amendment Act was passed, synchronized exactly with the hard times which caused the law to be felt as a great grievance, and, in its earlier years, drew most of its attacks on existing conditions from the complaints of those who suffered from the restrictions of the new system. If one cause was more important than any other in detaching the working classes who followed the Chartist banner from the general forces of Radicalism with which they had previously been associated, it was this Act and the defense of it by Radicals. How complete the alienation of the two classes was, and what bitterness it engendered, can be shown from J. Bronterre O'Brien's characterization of the conduct of the reformed Parliament and his estimate of the motives of its leaders:

What was the first act of that Reformed Parliament? The Coercion Bill for Ireland. What was the last act of the first session? The New Poor Law for England. Why did that base Parliament pass both these acts? To place the laboring classes of both countries at the feet of the rich assassins, who rob, brutalize, and enslave the populations of both. It is in the nature of things that the middle classes must be worse than any other part of the community.[2]

[1] *Hansard*, 3d series, vol. lxii, pp. 1376-81.
[2] *McDouall's Chartist and Republican Journal*, July 31, 1841.

CHAPTER II

THE HIGH TIDE OF CHARTISM

THE strength of the Chartist movement at different times is not easy to measure, for, like most popular agitations, it had periods of intense activity varied by intervals of comparative quiescence. On at least three occasions the movement showed sufficient strength to alarm the government and the conservative public. The first phase of the agitation culminated in the attack by an armed band of Chartists under John Frost and other leaders; the second in the wholesale strikes in the manufacturing districts of Lancashire and other northern counties in the summer of 1842; the third in the demonstration of April 10, 1848, when London was garrisoned by a special army of police constables to prevent disorder in connection with the presentation of the Chartist petition to Parliament. It need not be assumed that the real strength of the movement was greatest on these three occasions, but unquestionably it was then most evident. Each of these periods coincided with a more or less serious industrial crisis, just as the whole movement fell in a period of general industrial depression.

The strength of the movement in 1839 is evidenced by the great petition of that year, which boasted 1,280,000 signatures, collected in more than five hundred public meetings held in 214 towns and villages of Great Britain.[1] The degree of public interest in Chartism revealed by this num-

[1] *Hansard*, 3d series, vol. xlviii, p. 223.

ber of signatures was remarkable, for, after making all reasonable deductions for fraudulent signatures and the signatures of those who, as women, would not be enfranchised by the Charter, it is probable that the petition represented a far more numerous constituency than did the House of Commons which refused to consider it.[1]   But the two years following 1839 were marked by comparative inactivity, due in part no doubt to the prosecutions instituted by the government consequent upon the disorders of that year. The *Annual Register* records that, in the earlier part of 1841, " the hopes or apprehensions of the public were no longer excited by the prospect of any further extension of political rights; the outcry for the ballot, or an enlargement of the suffrage, had almost ceased." [2]   But as winter approached, agitation became intense and meetings were held throughout Great Britain to collect signatures for another great National Petition, demanding the six points of the Charter and repeal of the legislative union with Ireland, and setting forth a long list of popular grievances which seemed to the petitioners to justify their demands.

The monster petition of 1839 was completely eclipsed by the size of the one presented in 1842. This petition was signed by 3,315,752 persons,[3] showing an increase of nearly 160 per cent over the support accorded to the Chartist cause in 1839.   Thomas Duncombe presented it to the House of Commons on May 2, 1842, and on the following day the question of its reception was debated at great length. In spite of the support of many of the Radicals, the request for a hearing was denied by a majority of 238.[4]   It seemed

---

[1] *Cf. supra*, p. 21.

[2] *Annual Register*, vol. lxxxiii, p. 2.

[3] *Morning Herald*, cited in *Hansard*, 3d series, vol. lxiii, p. 29.

[4] *Hansard*, 3d series, vol. lxiii, pp. 13-91, gives the text of the debate.

evident that the Chartists could not by mere petitioning, no matter in what numbers, win any of their demands from the government. Whigs and Tories alike remained unconverted by the demonstration, and the *Times* spoke the mind of the conservative portion of the British public when it declared editorially that the size of the petition was quite irrelevant:

We are content with the more simple belief that the great question to be settled by the House of Commons, and by every one else who has either authority or influence over the course of legislation, is not how the people shall be fully represented, but how they shall be well governed; that governments do not rest on the consent of the people, but simply on their own established existence—that the powers *that be* have a claim upon our allegiance because *they are*.[1]

The distribution of the signatures to the petition of 1842 shows very clearly in what parts of the nation Chartism was strongest.[2]   London with its suburbs contributed about 200,000, Manchester nearly half as many (99,680), Newcastle and its suburbs about 92,000 or only a little fewer than Manchester, other factory towns very much in proportion to population. The country districts of Yorkshire and Lancashire contributed their share, but the Chartists as a whole were shown to be distinctly an urban class.   Scotland was strongly Chartist, at least in the manufacturing districts.   Glasgow and Lanarkshire produced 78,062 signatures.   Throughout Great Britain over four hundred towns or villages were represented by signatures to the petition. The number of Chartist " locals " had grown with surprising rapidity.   Northampton had nearly a dozen Chartist

[1] *Times*, May 3, 1842, italics in the original.

[2] For the signatures to the petition by localities, see *Hansard*, 3d series, vol. lxii, p. 1375.

associations in 1842, whereas in 1839 it had only two or three;[1] South Lancashire had eleven such organizations in 1840, and forty-five in 1842.[2] Of course not all the supporters of the petition were in the strictest sense active members of the Chartist party, but Duncombe estimated that " nearly 100,000 adults of the industrious portion of the community lay aside one penny per week of their wages for the purpose of carrying on and keeping up agitation in favor of their claim to the elective franchise." [3]

During the winter of 1841-2 the rise of Chartist agitation was paralleled by the increasing misery of the working classes. In spite of the efforts of the Poor Law commissioners to reduce pauperism by stringent work-house regulations, the amount expended for the poor increased annually from a minimum per capita rate of 5s. 5d. in the year 1836-7 to 6s. 1¾d. in 1841-2 and 6s. 5¼d. in 1842-3.[4] The percentage of the population of England and Wales in receipt of poor relief rose to nine and one-half in the year 1842-3.[5] A study of the condition of the poor in individual districts shows the same degree of destitution that is indicated by the poor-rate for the country as a whole. In Stockport, during the year 1842, eight shillings were paid for poor relief to every pound paid in rental.[6] In Leeds, according to the *London Sun* [7] men were trying to support themselves on 11¼d. per week. A private survey of 1003 work-

[1] Gammage, *History of the Chartist Movement*, p. 213.

[2] *English Chartist Circular*, vol. ii, p. 95.

[3] *Hansard*, 3d series, vol. lxiii, p. 20.

[4] *Parliamentary Papers*, 1852 (1461), xxiii, 1 *et seq.*

[5] Nicholls, *History of the English Poor Law*, vol. ii, p. 390.

[6] Engels, *Condition of the Working Class*, p. 87.

[7] Cited in Lester, *Condition and Fate of England* (New York, 1842 vol. ii, p. 39.

ingmen's families at Bolton-le-Moors in December, 1841, showed an average of less than 1s. 2½d. per head per week for food, clothing and all other expenses except rent.[1] More than half of these families had goods in pawn. In Paisley fifteen thousand persons were in receipt of poor relief.[2] In the woolen districts of Wiltshire the independent laborer received less than two-thirds the minimum support accorded to paupers in the workhouses.[3]

Indirect evidence of the poverty of the country is afforded by a study of the statistics of emigration and of marriage. The number of emigrants from the United Kingdom increased from only 33,222 in 1838 to 118,592 in 1841 and 128,344 in 1842.[4] The number of marriages suffered a steady decline from 1589 per 100,000 in 1839 to 1473 in 1842.[5] The significance of the decrease in the proportion of marriages is well expressed in the report: " The number of marriages in a nation perhaps fluctuates independently of external causes, but it is a fair deduction from the facts, that the marriage returns in England point out periods of prosperity, present in part, but future, expected, anticipated, in still greater part." [6] If this contention is sound, then from 1839 to 1842 the mass of the people were increasingly apprehensive of future want.

Parliament and the ministry of Sir Robert Peel were far from indifferent to the extent of the distress in the manufacturing districts. Even the royal address, which is always the most optimistic and conservative of sources for

---

[1] *Hansard*, 3d series, vol. lx, p. 259.

[2] *Ibid.*, p. 178.

[3] Martineau, *History of the Thirty Years' Peace*, vol. iv, pp. 155-6.

[4] Nicholls, *op. cit.*, p. 439.

[5] *Parliamentary Papers*, 1847-8 (967), xxv, 1 *et seq.*, p. v.

[6] *Ibid.*, p. xxiii.

the economic condition of the United Kingdom,[1] stated in February that Her Majesty had " observed with deep regret the continued distress in the manufacturing districts of the country," and added that the " sufferings and privations which have resulted from it have been borne with exemplary patience and fortitude." [2] In May a formal letter was sent by order of Her Majesty to His Grace the Archbishop of Canterbury, recommending, in view of the fact that " many of the Working Classes have suffered and continue to suffer, severe distress," that " the Ministers in each parish do effectually excite the parishioners to a liberal contribution, which shall be collected the week following at their respective dwellings by the Churchwardens or Overseers of the Poor in each Parish." [3] Beyond the extension of poor relief and the admonitions already mentioned to the rich to be " liberal " and to the poor to endure their want with " patience and fortitude ", the government did little to relieve the situation, although Sir Robert Peel decided that the time was ripe to make a slight revision of the Corn Laws with a view to checking speculation in foodstuffs, and also to make up a heavy deficit in the revenue by the imposition of an income tax of seven pence in the pound.   This income tax was at first intended to be levied for three years only, but it has been one of the sources of British revenue ever since.

The revision of the duties on grain [4] was also chiefly important in its relation to the future.   It involved

---

[1] This is, obviously, because the address represents the views of the ministry, whose policies would be held responsible for unusually hard times.

[2] *Annual Register*, vol. lxxxiv, p. 4.

[3] *Parliamentary Papers*, 1842 (383), xxvii, 57-8.

[4] By the 5 and 6 Vict., c. 14.

comparatively little change and it bitterly disappointed the free-traders in Parliament, but it was the beginning of the premier's concessions to the Anti-Corn Law League. A comparison of the new wheat schedule with the old will show something of the scope of the measure. The principle of both laws was the sliding scale, that is, as grain advanced in price in England the duty upon imported grain was decreased. Under the old rate when wheat sold at less than sixty shillings the quarter a duty of twenty-seven shillings was imposed on each quarter. For each additional shilling in price the duty was lessened one shilling until at sixty-seven shillings it was fixed at twenty shillings and eightpence. Above this point, the duty was lessened more rapidly, so that when wheat sold for seventy-three shillings, the duty was only two shillings and eightpence. If wheat sold for more than seventy-three shillings a flat rate of one shilling the quarter was imposed. By the new law the variation in the sliding scale was made more gradual. A duty of twenty shillings was imposed when wheat was less than fifty-one shillings the quarter, a nineteen shillings duty if from fifty-one to fifty-two shillings the quarter, an eighteen shillings duty if from fifty-two to fifty-five shillings the quarter, and from this point to sixty-six shillings the quarter the duty lessened by one shilling for each rise in price of equal amount. The duty was again uniform for prices from sixty-six to sixty-nine shillings the quarter, and then decreased more gradually till the price stood at seventy-three shillings, above which point the old one-shilling duty was retained.

As the summer in 1842 approached, discontent became keener and its expression more violent. On June fifth a meeting was held on Enfield Moor near Blackburn at which many appeared with firearms, and Marsden of Bolton threatened an armed deputation to Buckingham Palace to

obtain the Charter.[1]   But the great strike in August, which
was later " captured " by the Chartists and turned to political purposes, began as a simple protest against wage reductions.   The nailers near Wolverhampton had their wages
reduced by ten per cent and were, in addition, employed
only on a half-time basis.[2]   Similar conditions existed in
the collieries, where a strike or " turnout " followed upon
a reduction in wages of threepence a day.[3]   In the neighborhood of the Tyne the ship carpenters struck when their
pay was reduced early in August to twenty-one shillings a
week.[4]   On the fourth and fifth of August a great strike
of spinners and weavers began at Ashton.[5]   During the following week armed mobs invaded Manchester and the other
big factory towns.[6]   Wherever they went they " turned
out " the operatives, forcing even those who wished to remain at work to join them, put out the fires of steam engines,
drew plugs from the boilers, and intimidated the authorities.
Estimates in the *Times* placed the number of men thrown
out of work by the great turn-out as from fifty to eighty
thousand.[7]   Serious riots occurred at Stockport, at Preston
and in Staffordshire, but on the whole the strike, considering its extent, was remarkably orderly.   A typical report,
from Rochdale on the fifteenth of August, states that " a
few boys have threatened and begged and entered some
shops, but they have been reproved by the men." [8]   The

[1] *Annual Register*, vol. lxxxiv, pt. ii, p. 102.
[2] *Times*, July 28, 1842.
[3] *Ibid.*, Aug. 1, 1842.
[4] *Ibid.*, Aug. 9, 1842.
[5] *Annual Register*, op. cit., p. 133 *et seq.*
[6] Gammage, *History of the Chartist Movement*, pp. 217-25.
[7] *Times*, Aug. 12, 1842.
[8] *Ibid.*, Aug. 17, 1842.

textile operatives on the twenty-fifth of the month published a list of their demands, which included a wages schedule similar to that existing in 1840, a ten-hour day " or less," the employment of men as well as women and children in the weaving department, and weekly payments of wages.[1]

This industrial movement was quickly turned by the Chartists into a political demonstration. As early as the seventh of August a mass meeting on Mottram Moor had resolved not to end the strike until the Charter was won.[2] Three hundred and fifty-eight labor delegates, chiefly from the manufacturing districts of Lancashire and the West Riding of Yorkshire, met in Manchester on the twelfth, and three hundred and twenty of them voted to continue the turnout until the Charter was the law of the land.[3] It was further resolved to make the strike general throughout the country. The executive committee of the National Chartist Association issued a formal proclamation to the striking workers on August sixteenth, as follows:

Peace, law, and order have prevailed on our side; let them be revered until your brethren in Scotland, Wales, and Ireland, are informed of your resolution; and when a universal holiday prevails—which will be the case in eight days—then of what use will bayonets be against public opinion? . . . Our machinery is all arranged, and your cause will in three days be impelled onward by all the intellect we can summon to its aid. Therefore whilst you are peaceful, be firm; whilst you are orderly, make all be so likewise; and whilst you look to the law, remember that you had no voice in making it, and are therefore slaves to the will, the law, and the price of your masters. All officers of the Association are called upon to aid and assist

[1] *Times*, Aug. 26, 1842.
[2] Gammage, *op. cit.*, p. 217.
[3] *Ibid.*, p. 218.

in the peaceful extension of the movement, and to forward all moneys for the use of the delegates who may be expressed over the country.[1]

It is evident from the tone of the proclamation that the Chartists were determined not to let such an exceptional opportunity as the great turnout afforded fail through any ill-timed violence. Feargus O'Connor made this plain in a public letter, in the course of which he advised: " Let no blood be shed. Let no life be destroyed. Let no property be consumed. Let us, in God's name, set an example to the world of what moral power is capable of effecting." [2]

In the latter part of August and throughout September the striking workingmen returned, either without gaining their aims or else compromising on local arrangements with their employers. Before the end of September, the *Stockport Chronicle* reported that the whole of the turnout operatives had returned to work.[3] Four of the members of the Chartist executive were arrested, because the address to the striking workingmen issued by the National Chartist Association was regarded as treasonable.[4] McDouall, who was probably its author, received warning in time and escaped to France. O'Connor was among the leaders apprehended by the authorities. As a final result of the special commission in Staffordshire, fifty-four persons were sentenced to transportation, eleven of these for life, the rest for more than seven years; while 154 were sentenced to various terms of imprisonment.[5] The vigorous official action after the political strike had subsided contrasts

---

[1] Gammage, *History of the Chartist Movement*, pp. 218-9.

[2] *Times*, Aug. 22, 1842.

[3] Cited in the *Times*, Sept. 29, 1842.

[4] Gammage, *op. cit.*, pp. 228-31.

[5] *Annual Register*, vol. lxxxiv, pt. ii, p. 163.

strongly with the inactivity of the authorities during its course. To be sure, the government sent troops and artillery to the manufacturing districts and a royal proclamation, dated August 13, 1842, offered indemnity and a reward of fifty pounds to informers.[1] But both the local magistrates and the military commanders seemed to feel that so long as the strikers refrained from the destruction of life and property it was better to permit them to stop the mills. Complaints of this inactivity, such as the following report from Bury, were not infrequent:

Notwithstanding the promise of the magistrates to give the millowners protection, the mob was not interfered with either by the police or the military, though there were 110 soldiers in the place; and notice had been given to the magistrates of the approach of the mob. No damage was committed by the mob which entered Bury; and, after effecting their purpose of stopping the mills, proceeded on to Bolton.[2]

The failure of the turnout of August 1842 to obtain either the Charter or the desired wages schedules, seems to have been due to two main causes. In the first place, a bad time was chosen, after a prolonged industrial depression when the strikers were practically without reserve funds to support themselves for any length of time and when employers were laying men off or working them only part time. Indeed, many Conservatives believed that the surprising weakness shown by the magistrates in the north of England in dealing with the turnouts was due to the fact that many of them were Whigs and free-traders who were not at all sorry to see a big political demonstration which would embarrass Sir Robert Peel's government and make it difficult to refuse the popular clamor for cheaper corn.

[1] *Times*, Aug. 15, 1842.   [2] *Ibid.*, Aug. 20, 1842.

Early in 1842 Cobden had suggested a refusal of taxes and
Bright a general closure of factories as possible means of
coercing the government.[1]   The manufacturers, who could
hope at best for little profit in such a year, were willing to
let their mills and factories be closed for a few weeks, and
they knew that the scanty resources of the strikers would
hardly permit them to prolong the turnout for a greater
length of time.   Many of the workingmen realized this,
and their consequent half-heartedness was the other important source of weakness to the strike.   The *Times* cleverly
compared the striking Chartists to any army of five hundred, drawn up in hollow square around 4500 prisoners,
claiming to be a force of five thousand.[2]   Some of the
strikers desired only the restoration of the old wages, others
did not wish to strike at all and did so only from coercion.
The fact that the strikers had to go in large bands from
mill to mill forcing the operatives to leave their work, shows
that many would rather have remained as they were.   The
majority of British workingmen would willingly have subscribed to the principles of the Chartists, but only a minority
of them would ever have endangered their livelihood in
such a doubtful enterprise as a general strike for manhood
suffrage.   As a demonstration the turnout was not in reality
a failure, for it showed the strength and numbers of the
discontented as they had never been shown before.   The
Stockport Chronicle gave as its opinion that never before in
history had there been " a cessation of labor so extensive,
simultaneous, and protracted," [3] while the *Times* reported
that never since Chartism became known had it been so
completely organized.[4]

[1] G. M. Trevelyan, *The Life of John Bright* (London, 1914), pp. 76-78.

[2] *Times*, Aug. 22, 1842.

[3] Cited in the *Times*, Sept. 29, 1842.   [4] *Times*, Aug. 12, 1842.

During a large part of the year 1842 the Chartist cause was much strengthened by the prospect of a good understanding with some of the middle-class Radicals. In February one petition combined a demand for Corn Law repeal with that for the Charter.[1] In April a conference was arranged at Birmingham between the Chartists and a middle-class organization for " complete suffrage " led by the Rev. Joseph Sturge.[2] Among the Chartists who attended were Lovett, Collins, Vincent and O'Brien. The Chartists throughout the first day's session were inclined to suspect the sincerity of their new allies, but, as the representatives of the Complete Suffrage Association accepted one after another of the six points, their enthusiasm increased until on the second day (April 6, 1842) O'Brien volunteered the information that he " had never been in any society, composed even exclusively of working men, in which he had found the democratic spirit more thoroughly developed." [3] Not all of the points of the Charter were carried without discussion. Some of the Complete Suffrage representatives doubted the value of annual Parliaments,[4] of the ballot and of the payment of members of the House of Commons by the state. The absolute denunciation of the physical force party and its methods called out some protest by the Chartists,[5] and O'Brien objected particularly to the attack on the " Feargusites " or followers of Feargus O'Connor.[6]

---

[1] Engels, *Condition of the Working Class in 1844*, p. 231.

[2] *Report of the Proceedings at the Conference of Delegates of the Middle and Working Classes, held at Birmingham, April 5, 1842, and three following days* (London, 1842).

[3] *Ibid.*, p. 38.

[4] The Rev. T. Spencer made the interesting suggestion of the recall as a possible substitute for annual Parliaments. *Report of the Birmingham Conference*, p. 17.

[5] *Ibid.*, p. 7.   [6] *Ibid.*, p. 11.

But the two factions in the conference reached substantial agreement upon all questions of aim and policy until the question of the name of the new organization arose.[1] Lovett and the other Chartists insisted that, having adopted all the points of the Charter, the conference should adopt the name as well; the Complete Suffragists wished some other name to be chosen, regarding the old term as too much associated with the physical-force methods of the past. The delegates could reach no agreement upon the point, and wisely determined to let the question remain unsettled until December. Some practical rules and methods of action were provisionally agreed upon, the conference adjourned,[2] and the Chartists for the first and last time entered upon a campaign with a considerable middle-class support.

The friendship subsisting between the Sturgeites and the Chartists bore valuable fruit in the Parliamentary contests of the summer. Joseph Sturge appeared as a candidate for the borough of Nottingham in August. Vincent, Cooper, O'Connor and " great numbers of operatives . . brought in by the Chartist leaders from the neighboring villages, and from more distant towns "[3] gathered to support his candidacy. Both O'Connor and Vincent made speeches in support of his nomination.[4] Sturge's opponent, a Mr. Walter, who based his campaign chiefly upon his opposition to the new Poor Law, was returned over Sturge by the narrow margin of eighty-four votes.[5] At Southampton[6]

---

[1] *Report of the Birmingham Conference*, p. 55.

[2] It may be noted, parenthetically, that a reading of the report of the Conference leaves one with the irresistible impression that the debates recorded therein compare favorably in quality with the Parliamentary debates recorded in *Hansard*.

[3] *Times*, Aug. 4, 1842.   [4] *Times*, Aug. 5, 1842.

[5] Walter, 1885; Sturge, 1801. *Times*, Aug. 8, 1842.

[6] *Ibid.*, Aug. 9, 1842.

and Ipswich [1] Chartist candidates polled heavy votes, and at several elections the Chartists showed their real strength among the unenfranchised by attending the polls in a body and electing their candidates on the first show of hands, although the official returns, of course, took no account of these demonstrations. But in October the Chartists won a positive, though small, success in electing sixteen police commissioners out of seventy-two in the town of Dundee.[2] In 1841 they had been able to elect only seven.

In September Joseph Sturge suggested a basis for the second conference between the Complete Suffrage party and the Chartists.[3] He proposed that electors and non-electors should return equal numbers of delegates, that the smaller towns should have two representatives apiece, the more considerable boroughs (of five thousand and upwards population) four apiece, while such important centers of radical activity as London, Manchester, Birmingham, Liverpool, Edinburgh and Glasgow, should each have six. His plan was adopted, and Sturge himself was unanimously chosen to preside over the conference when it met in Birmingham on December 27, 1842.[4] Letters were read from W. Sharman Crawford, M. P. and Daniel O'Connell. Both expressed their approval of the Charter, but both declined to enter the Conference—Sharman Crawford because he could be of more service to the democratic cause as an independent friend of the Chartists in Parliament than as a member of the party, while O'Connell held aloof because of

[1] *Times*, Aug. 17, 1842.

[2] *Memoranda of the Chartist Agitation in Dundee* (anonymous, un-dated), p. 66.

[3] *English Chartist Circular*, vol. ii, p. 128.

[4] Gammage, *History of the Chartist Movement*, pp. 241-5; *Times*, Dec. 28, 1842.

the violence and narrowness of the "physical-force" faction.[1] T. Beggs, a Nottingham delegate, presented a series of resolutions providing that the conference endorse the "six points"; favor "such means only for obtaining the legislative recognition of them as are of a strictly just, peaceful, legal, and constitutional character"; refuse to consider irrelevant matters; and, while ready to consider any document laid before it, take as the basis for discussion the Bill of Rights prepared by the council of the National Complete Suffrage Union.[2]

The Chartists at once attacked the last proposal and William Lovett moved to substitute the Charter as the basis for discussion. The two measures were substantially identical, as both parties to the conference admitted, but there was an absolute deadlock over the term "Chartist." Lovett, as leader of the Chartist faction at the conference, proposed in the interest of harmony that both bills be withdrawn or both be considered clause by clause.[3] But all attempts at conciliation failed, and Lovett's original motion carried by the decisive majority of 193 to 94. Thereupon Joseph Sturge resigned the chair and many of the Complete Suffragists, including the ex-Chartist leader Henry Vincent, seceded. The two bodies then met separately, transacted necessary business, and adjourned on the thirtieth.[4] Meeting separately, the Chartists passed a resolution condemning the conduct of the Sturgeites in abandoning the Conference.

On the face of it, the conference had split over nothing. Sturgeites and O'Connorites quite agreed as to political principles and there was no irreconcilable difference upon ques-

---

[1] *Times*, Dec. 29, 1842.

[2] *Ibid.*

[3] Wm. Lovett, *Life and Struggles in Pursuit of Bread, Knowledge, and Freedom* (London, 1876), p. 284.

[4] *Times*, Jan. 2, 1843.

tions of detail and of party tactics.   But the two organizations were unable to fuse because of the class antipathy latent in the ranks of each.   As one of the delegates, Mr. Heyworth of Liverpool, correctly phrased the issue: " the fact was the present contest was for ' who shall be your leaders? ' " [1]   We have testimony from both Chartists [2] and Complete Suffragists [3] that the unwillingness of the latter to take any part in an organization in which O'Connor and his disciples were powerful was the real cause of the schism. The Complete Suffrage party wished that the new organization should abandon the Chartist name because of the traditions of violence and class antagonism with which it was associated, accept middle-class leadership and progress along the lines of constitutional agitation in friendship and alliance with the Anti-Corn Law League.   The Chartists, as we have seen, had a very different conception of the form and purpose of their propaganda.   They desired a party organized and led by workingmen and directed ultimately to social and economic ends through the medium of the Charter.   They did not refuse an alliance with the middle-class Radicals, but they were unwilling to make any concession, even of name, to maintain it, because they had an ingrained distrust of their new allies and viewed every divergence on their part from the strictest party orthodoxy as an attempt to betray the democratic cause.   Moreover, the Charter for which they had struggled for so many years, had acquired a sentimental value in their eyes, and they could not consent to abandon the name even to secure its substance.   It meant to them all that the word " Socialist " means to many a radical workingman today.

[1] *Times*, Dec. 30, 1842.

[2] Lovett, *op. cit.*, p. 285.

[3] Henry Richard, *Memoirs of Joseph Sturge* (1864), p. 318.

But both Chartists and Complete Suffragists realized the injurious effect of the broken conference at Birmingham upon their future efforts. Thomas Cooper gave as his opinion: " That Birmingham Conference ruined the prospects of Chartists; and the Complete Suffrage party never made any headway in the country." [1]   It is true that Joseph Sturge continued the struggle for a few years, but without success, as his organization was now divorced from those sources of popular enthusiasm which alone could have then effected such a sweeping political reform as he desired.   In 1844 he contested the borough of Birmingham on a manhood suffrage platform, but received only 350 votes.[2]   He remained an advocate of manhood suffrage but turned his attention more and more to the anti-slavery movement and to peace propaganda.   For the Chartists, the conference marked not only the end of the middle-class alliance, but the beginning of the dissolution of the party itself into contending and jealous factions wasting their best efforts in thwarting each other's activities.

[1] *Life of Thomas Cooper*, p. 228.
[2] Richard, *op. cit.*, pp. 320-322.

CHAPTER III

The Disintegration of the Chartist Movement

ANOTHER long period of discouragement and inactivity
followed the failure of the political strike and the Birmingham conference. So little interest was taken in the affairs
of the party that the next Chartist convention, summoned
originally for April 1843, did not meet until the fifth of
September.[1] This convention, unlike the conference of the
previous year, contained none but strict Chartists and the
only prominent leaders present were adherents of Feargus
O'Connor. O'Connor's ascendancy within the party, due
in part to his own striking personality and in part to the
hopes aroused by his plan for resettling the town laborers
upon the land, was further confirmed by the dependent position in which the newly elected executive found itself.
O'Connor had up to that time refused to serve on the executive at all, and had even proposed to limit its power by
the clumsy device of a council of thirteen, chosen by public
meetings, to act as a check on the executive, audit its accounts and countersign its public documents.[2] But O'Connor
as a member of that body found a surer method of controll-
ing it through its failure to get adequate financial support
from the public. The National Chartist Association was
so poor that it could not pay the salaries of the nine lecturers
appointed by the executive, or even of the executive officials

[1] Gammage, *History of the Chartist Movement*, p. 248.
[2] *Ibid.*, p. 247.

who appointed them.[1]   O'Connor made up these recurrent deficits by loans from his considerable private fortune.

In March 1843 Feargus O Connor and fifty-eight other persons were indicted on nine different counts in connection with the great Lancashire strike.[2]   Twenty-one were acquitted by the jury, seven dismissed in the course of the trial, sixteen found guilty on the fourth count and fifteen on the fifth.   But the accused conducted their cases with marked ability, and the whole proceedings were finally quashed on the technical ground that the indictments did not specify the locality of the alleged offences.   O'Connor's reprint of the case [3] was dedicated to Justice Baron Rolfe, who presided over the trials and showed marked consideration to the accused.   Thomas Cooper was not, however, so fortunate as O'Connor.   Acquitted of the charge of arson, he was rearrested on the charge of sedition and received a sentence of two years' imprisonment.[4]   While Cooper was in prison he improved his time by writing his most famous poem, *The Purgatory of Suicides*, a work that introduced him to the literary public and to many of the most distinguished British authors, including Charles Kingsley.[5]

The triumphant acquittal of O'Connor, and the imprisonment or exile of a number of Chartists who might have been his rivals for party leadership, left him in a position of unusual strength.   Nevertheless, O'Con-

---

[1] Gammage, *op. cit.*, p. 251.

[2] *Ibid.*, pp. 231-41.

[3] *Trial of Feargus O'Connor and Fifty-eight others at Lancaster* (1843).

[4] Gammage, *op. cit.*, p. 240.

[5] It has been asserted that Thomas Cooper was the original of "Alton Locke" in Kingsley's novel of that name, and that the dictatorial and eccentric journalist "O'Flynn" was drawn from the character of Feargus O'Connor. *Cf.* Dierlamm, *Die Flugschriftenliteratur der Chartistenbewegung*, p. 100.

nor suffered one serious setback during the years of his leadership. The Anti-Corn Law League was very active during the crisis of 1842 and the years which followed, and O'Connor, as leader of the Chartists and opponent of the theory of free trade, felt obliged to send a challenge to its leaders for a debate on the question of repeal. At last he and two other Chartists, Harrison and McGrath, met Bright and Cobden in a public debate at Northampton on August 5, 1844.[1] O'Connor was a brilliant orator but a somewhat inconclusive debater and the Chartists themselves admitted that the honors of the occasion were wholly with the League. Gammage even went so far as to describe the debate as the greatest victory the League ever obtained. It was a severe blow to the prestige of the Chartists and especially of their leader.

Neither the Chartists nor the Anti-Corn Law League won many recruits for two or three years after the stormy days of 1842. But the Chartists suffered much more than the League since they lacked the financial resources necessary to keep their propaganda alive during a period of comparative public indifference. The most important of Chartist publications, O'Connor's *Northern Star*, proved a heavy drain on the fortune of its publisher, and was transferred from Leeds to London in the hope of improving its circulation.[2] At the very time when the best efforts of every Chartist were needed to rouse the country, the party was torn by internal dissensions and revolts against the dictatorship assumed by O'Connor. It was wholly unprepared to meet with united strength the next great opportunity for successful agitation.

The quarrel with the Anti-Corn Law League and

---

[1] Gammage, *op. cit.*, pp. 253-5.
[2] *Life of Thomas Cooper*, p. 271.

with the Complete Suffragists under Joseph Sturge was unfortunate enough, for it effectually prevented any such
union between the working classes and the powerful Radical
party which triumphed over the aristocracy in 1832. But
even as a purely proletarian organization Chartism might
have accomplished much if its various elements had been
able to work harmoniously. At no one time, however,
were all the Chartist leaders in substantial agreement as to
the proper aims and methods of the party. Even in the
summer of 1842, when the Chartist factions were most
nearly united and an agreement with the middle-class Radicals seemed not beyond the reach of hope, riots occurred
between the followers of O'Connor and those of Joseph
Raynor Stephens, the opponent of the New Poor Law, over
the nomination of Sturge for the borough of Nottingham.[1]

The first wedge that split the united movement was the
conflict between Feargus O'Connor and William Lovett.
The London Working Men's Association adopted a resolution to include in their active membership only those who
were themselves of the working class. It was charged that
the sole purpose of this action was to exclude O'Connor,
who was a rather wealthy landowner and boasted descent
from the ancient kings of Ireland.[2] In return, the educa-
tional and social reforms advocated by Lovett were attacked by O'Connor on the ground that they confused the
plain issue of the Charter with other questions such as popular education and the temperance movement. In the pages
of the *Northern Star* O'Connor dubbed his opponents
" knowledge Chartists." [3] Lovett admitted that he had been
accused of trying " to make teetotalism another point in

[1] *Times*, Aug. 4, 1842.
[2] Gammage, *op. cit.*, p. 13.
[3] *Ibid.*, pp. 195-7.

the Charter."[1] In 1843 Lovett refused to accept office
in the National Charter Association because he found it
impossible to work in harmony with O'Connor.

Other secessions quickly followed. McDouall returned
from France to Scotland in 1845. On his return he suggested the formation of a separate Chartist organization
for Scotland, but O'Connor promptly attacked this proposal
as an attempt to break the unity of the movement.[2]
O'Connor managed to retain an autocratic control over the
National Charter Association, but the Association did not
succeed in gaining complete control of the movement.
Many Chartist locals refused entirely to submit themselves
to the guidance of the national organization.[3] Even
O'Connor's intimate disciples were readily alienated by his
jealousy of other leaders of the movement. Thomas
Cooper, for example, had been O'Connor's most ardent
lieutenant. His followers had even taken part in breaking
up the public meetings held by J. Bronterre O'Brien and
Joseph Sturge at a time when O'Connor opposed any alliance between Chartists and Complete Suffragists.[4] But
when Cooper had finished his term of imprisonment for his
share in the riotous demonstrations of 1842 he discovered
that O'Connor had published an attack upon him, and from
that time forth he refused to have anything to do with his
old leader.[5]

The Chartist division most frequently mentioned, at least
in secondary sources, was that between the leaders who re-
lied upon " moral force " to accomplish their aims, and those

[1] *English Chartist Circular*, vol. i, p. 9.

[2] Gammage, *op. cit.*, pp. 258-60.

[3] Schlüter, *Die Chartistenbewegung*, p. 219.

[4] Gammage, *op. cit.*, pp. 202-5.

[5] *Life of Thomas Cooper*, p. 271.

who trusted to " physical force." Lovett was the recognized champion of the former faction. The moral force Chartists believed that they could carry the Charter by means of public meetings, agitation, petitions and direct or indirect influence at the polls. The physical force Chartists held that sooner or later an armed insurrection would be necessary to force the government to yield. O'Connor was usually classed with this latter group, but not altogether justly. In 1839, to be sure, he was a man of violent counsels, but in the crises of 1842 and 1848 he advised moderation.[1] The *Nonconformist*, the organ of the Complete Suffrage Association, claimed him as an adherent of the moral force section of the Chartists.[2] His friend Julian Harney of the *Northern Star* stood somewhat more consistently for the methods of physical force, and Stephens during his early crusade against the New Poor Law was completely a revolutionist.

But it is easy to exaggerate the importance of this division between the moral force and the physical force sections of the party. There was, as a matter of fact, no clear line of demarcation between the two types of method or between the men who inclined to one or the other. The Chartist convention of 1839 suggested many measures which did not involve armed revolt and yet can hardly be considered as exercising purely " moral force." The general strike was one of these proposals; others were abstinence from excisable articles, exclusive dealing with Chartist tradesmen, and a run on the banks.[3] It is largely a matter of definition whether we count an enforced turnout, such as that in August 1842, a physical force measure or not. Moreover,

---

[1] *Cf. supra*, p. 69; *infra*, p. 99.

[2] *The Nonconformist*, June 8, 1842.

[3] Gammage, *op. cit.*, p. 109.

Chartists held various positions on the subject at various times. Thomas Cooper, for example, was almost as inconsistent as O'Connor. In 1842 he stirred the Staffordshire potteries districts into open revolt—although no doubt the strikers went much further than he intended that they should—and was sentenced to two year's imprisonment for his part in the affair. In 1846 he moved the following resolution:

That the Convention deplores the acts of violence which have filled the public mind with an aversion to Chartism, and hereby records its abandonment and disavowal of the doctrine of physical force, and its resolve to seek the establishment of the People's Charter as a statute of the realm solely by peaceable, moral, and constitutional means.[1]

The true importance of the dispute between moral force and physical force sections of the party, was not that this was an especially serious cause of friction or that it classified Chartists into distinct camps. It may be considered rather as a symptom of schism than a cause of it. The real difficulty was that at no time could the party agree upon any definite plan of action. The same tendencies to moderation or to violence existed in 1839 as in 1848 or even later; the first cause of quarrel, the quarrel about methods of agitation, was born with Chartism and did not end until the movement, too, had disappeared. A far more acute and bitter dispute raged over the land plan of Feargus O'Connor.

O'Connor, discouraged at the slow progress of Chartist agitation, decided to create a National Land Company for the purpose of purchasing private estates and dividing them into peasant holdings. He had always favored an agricultural rather than an industrial basis as the proper foundation for a free society, and he found in his position of

[1] *Gammage*, op. cit., p. 275.

leadership in the Chartist party a great opportunity to realize this favorite dream.   He thought, too, that the interest
in his great agrarian experiment would in turn react upon
the fortunes of the Chartist movement and reawaken interest in it and in his newspaper.   Briefly, the plan was as
follows.[1]   Whoever desired a holding would buy a certain
number of shares in the Company and pay cash down
£1 6s. for each share (as the rate was fixed in the first circular),[2] and among the subscribers a certain number would
be chosen by ballot for the first chance at a farm.[3]   Those
fortunate enough to win the right to immediate possession
would be settled by the Company on holdings prepared and
fitted for occupancy and receive a small loan of money
besides to start them on their new undertaking.   For each
share they had subscribed they would receive one acre of
land and £7 10s. advance.   Upon them would rest the obli-
gation to repay to the Company the value of the land and
cottage, and the money advanced, the payment taking the
form of rent, first fixed at 5 per cent per annum.[4]   The
money so returned to the Company would be spent in buying up more estates, preparing more soil, building new cottages, and advancing money to those who were next to be
settled upon the holdings of the Company.   This process
would continue until all subscribers were established under
the system as landholders.

Feargus O'Connor had the Irishman's enthusiasm for

[1] The fullest account of O'Connor's enterprise is in the six *Reports
on the National Land Company*, when it underwent Parliamentary investigation.   Reference must also be made to *The Labourer*, a periodical edited by O'Connor and Ernest Jones in the interest of the land
scheme.

[2] *Parliamentary Papers*, 1847-8 (398), xix, 1 *et seq.*, p. 5.

[3] Ibid., 1847-8 (420), xix, 73 *et seq.*, p. 31.

[4] *Labourer*, vol. iii, p. 57.

the small farm.   He detested city life and industrial occu-
pations as essentially artificial and hoped that his plan
would call the British workingman " back to the land."   If
he were successful in this, he expected the further benefit
that the manufacturers would be compelled to establish
a very high scale of wages to induce anyone to stay in
the manufacturing towns and work for wages who might
enjoy independence and prosperity on his own land in the
country.[1]   In the *Northern Star*, January 30, 1847, he
estimated that three acres would be amply sufficient to support a family.   Not only could the farmer make a good
living from a small plot of ground but he need spend but
little on improvements.   O'Connor believed that " spade
husbandry " paid better than farming with the improved
agricultural machinery which was coming into use.[2]   He
favored also reducing the use of draught animals to a minimum.   On this very economical basis, he thought he might
be able to locate 24,000 families within five years.[3]

The defects of O'Connor's land plan are obvious.   He
never took into consideration the difficulty a town population, many of whom had never lived in the country, would
have in learning to become agriculturists.   He did not, apparently, realize that if his land plan really worked and
many estates were purchased it would cause a serious rise
in the price of land and make future purchases more costly.
He assumed that land could be bought in unlimited quanti-
ties at reasonable rates and that every beneficiary of the
National Land Company would make a successful farmer
and punctually repay his indebtedness.   In spite of the ela-

[1] F. O'Connor, *A Practical Work on the Management of Small Farms*
(1843), p. 9.

[2] *Ibid.*, pp. 39-46.

[3] *Labourer*, vol. i, p. 173.

borate calculations with which he filled *The Labourer*, few persons outside the Chartist movement and not all within it believed that prosperous farming was possible on so small a scale and with such primitive methods as O'Connor advocated.   These inherent weaknesses in the scheme were made worse by O'Connor's carelessness and inaccuracy in all financial matters.

The Land Company was first registered October 24, 1846.[1]   O'Connor was the chairman of the board of directors, and active also in the Land Bank which he established as an auxiliary to his enterprise.   The Company was capitalized at £130,000 or 100,000 shares.[2]   O'Connor had practically a free hand in managing the details of the plan; he could purchase land whenever he saw " any eligible offer." [3] This provision made it inevitable that the affairs of the Company would be inefficiently managed.   O'Connor even failed to furnish the authorities with the full data required by law for the proper registration of joint stock companies.[4] The scheme would speedily have collapsed, if its organizer had not been as able a promoter as he was incompetent as a director.   He agitated for his land plan even more ardently than he had ever done for the Charter and succeeded in interesting a sufficient number of his admirers to give the plan a good start.   On May 24, 1847, the Herringsgate estate, near Watford, was opened for settlement under the name of O'Connorville, and subscriptions increased to £3,500 and even £5,000 a week.[5]   By August, 1847, the land fund

---

[1] *Parliamentary Papers*, 1847-8 (398), xix, 1 *et seq.*, p. 3.   The appendix of the report gives the rules of the company.

[2] *Ibid.*, p. 50.

[3] *Ibid.*, p. 42.

[4] *Parliamentary Papers, op. cit.*, p. 12.

[5] Gammage, *op. cit.*, p. 283.

reached a sum of £50,000.[1]   Encouraged by the success of
O'Connorville, O'Connor purchased larger estates and ven-
tured in September of the same year to propose that the
government take over the National Land Company and re-
plant an English peasantry on an extensive scale.[2]

The land plan greatly added to the prestige of O'Connor
among the Chartists, and somewhat to the prestige of
Chartism among the workingmen.   But this advantage was
much more than counterbalanced by the harmful effect of
the division of opinion it introduced within the party ranks.
Many Chartists believed that it was in the highest degree
harmful to tie a political agitation to the fortunes of a
commercial enterprise.   They remembered how O'Connor
had read rivals out of the party for trying to saddle the
Chartist agitation with other reforms in which they had
an interest, and they accused him in turn with being " no
longer a ' five point ' Chartist, but a ' five acre ' Chartist." [3]
Others, who had no scruples about involving Chartism in en-
tangling alliances with other issues, none the less opposed
the land plan either from distrust of O'Connor or from a
conviction that the attempt to establish a peasant proprietorship in England was futile or reactionary.

J. Bronterre O'Brien filled the columns of his *National
Reformer* with attacks upon the land plan.   He pointed out
that a class of small landowners would be the best security
the government could desire for keeping the mass of the
people conservative.   " Every man," he wrote, " who joins
these land societies is practically enlisting himself on the
side of the Government against his own order." [4]   As a

---

[1] Gammage, *op. cit.*, p. 285.

[2] *Labourer*, vol. ii, p. 154.

[3] John Watkins, *Impeachment of Feargus O'Connor* (1843), p. 20.

[4] *National Reformer and Manx Weekly Review*, Jan. 9, 1847.

substitute for O'Connor's project, he advocated keeping the land in the hands of the state, to be let out (not sold) to the best advantage of the entire public.[1] Feargus O'Connor retaliated by filling the *Northern Star* with denunciations of the economic theories of O'Brien—land nationalization and a purely symbolic currency.[2] The breach was complete. In 1848, O'Brien said: " I know nothing of Mr. O'Connor; I have had nothing to do with him for the last six or seven years." [3]

Thomas Cooper was another formidable opponent of O'Connor's project. Not content with denouncing the land plan, he threatened to propose a series of resolutions in the Chartist convention of 1846 practically reading O'Connor out of the party. One of these resolutions read: " That this Convention regards Feargus O'Connor as unworthy the confidence of Chartists, and hereby warns British working men of the folly and danger of union with him." [4] Ernest Jones threatened Cooper with expulsion if he persisted in his attempt to present the resolutions, and the next morning Cooper was denied admission.[5] This high-handed act of exclusion discredited the faction loyal to O'Connor more than Cooper's resolutions could have done even if the convention had accepted them.

On the other hand, the supporters of O'Connor were wildly enthusiastic and would listen to no criticism. Their feeling was well indicated by Ernest Jones's poem on the purchase of O'Connorville:

---

[1] *National Reformer and Manx Weekly Review*, Oct. 3, 1846; *cf. supra*, pp. 42-3.

[2] Gammage, *op. cit.*, pp. 260-1, 267-9.

[3] *Times*, April 10, 1848.

[4] Gammage, *op. cit.*, pp. 272-5.

[5] *Ibid.*, p. 280.

"Has freedom whispered in his wistful ear,
  'Courage, poor slave! deliverance is *near*?'
Oh! She has breathed a summons sweeter still
  'Come! take your guerdon at O'Connorville!'"[1]

It is evident that to men who felt like this a land plan which meant immediate release from factory life was more important than a Charter which promised the same result in the indefinite future. O'Connor replied to his critics by appearing before a mass-meeting of his partisans in Manchester to defend his plan and seek a public vindication. He told his audience that his enemies had plotted to ruin him and even to kill him. " O'Connor tested public confidence to the utmost," wrote Gammage. " He said, ' I have now brought money with me to repay every shareholder in Manchester.' (Shouts of ' Nay, but we won't have it!'). ' Well, then, I'll spend it all.' (Cries of ' Do, and welcome!')."[2] No other Chartist leader could claim a following as devoted as O'Connor's and so none of the abler men of the party could displace him from the leadership.

In 1848 the National Land Company began to suffer from the mismanagement of O'Connor, the irregularity of its organization and the inability of the new farmers to make a living from their holdings, and Parliament ordered an investigation into its affairs. The Company had indeed accomplished something; it had built 250 dwellings and four schoolhouses, it had cleared, prepared and planted a large part of the purchased land.[3] But the Poor Law authorities had been informed that " all those who occupy the Land Company's allotments, with nothing more than the

---

[1] E. Jones, *Chartist Songs and Fugitive Pieces* (London, undated), p. 11. Italics as in the original.

[2] Gammage, *op. cit.*, p. 288.

[3] *Parliamentary Papers*, 1847-8 (420), xix, 73 *et seq.*, p. 21.

produce of their allotments to depend upon, will fail to
obtain a living," and the fear was expressed that this condition might "lead to serious and sudden burthens upon
the poor's rates of those parishes in which they acquire
land." [1] The purchases of the company to June, 1848, were
as follows: [2]

Estates Purchased.	Acreage.	Date of Contract.	Date of Completion of Purchase.	Purchase Money.
Herringsgate, near Watford	103	March, 1846	May, 1846	£2,344
Lowbands, near Gloucester	170	October, 1846	December, 1846	8,560
Minster Lovell, near Witney	297	June, 1847	August, 1847	10,878
Snig's End, near Gloucester	268	June, 1847	November, 1847	12,200
Dodford, near Bromsgrove	280	January, 1848	May, 1848	10,350
Mathon, near Worcester	500	July, 1847	Not completed	15,350

In the sixth Report on the National Land Company, dated
August 1, 1848, the committee of investigation summarized
the reasons for putting an end to the operations of the Company. Since O'Connor's enterprise bulks so large in the
later history of the Chartist movement, it may be well to
cite from this report at some length. [3] It found:

1. That the proposed additional provisions to the Friendly
Societies' Acts which are incorporated in the Bill, entitled
"A Bill to alter and amend an Act of the 9th and 10th years of
Her present Majesty, for the Amendment of the Laws relating
to Friendly Societies," will not include the National Land Com-
pany within those Acts.

2. That the National Land Company is not consistent with
the general principles upon which the Friendly Societies are
founded.

[1] *Parliamentary Papers*, 1847-8 (503), xix, 207 *et seq.*, p. 34.

[2] *Ibid.* (557), xix, 295 *et seq.*, p. 31.

[3] *Ibid.* (577), xix, 333 *et seq.*

3. That the National Land Company, as at present consti-
tuted, is an illegal scheme, and will not fulfil the expectations
held out by the Directors to the Shareholders.

4. That it appearing to this committee by the evidence of
several witnesses that the books of the proceedings of the
National Land Company, as well as the accounts of the Company, have been most imperfectly kept, and that the original
balance-sheets signed by the auditors of the Company have been
destroyed, and only three of those balance-sheets, for the
quarters ending the 29th of September and the 25th of December 1847, and the 25th of March 1848 respectively, have been
produced; but Mr. Feargus O'Connor having expressed an
opinion that an impression had gone abroad that the moneys
subscribed by the National Land Company had been applied
to his own benefit, this Committee are clearly of the opinion,
that although the accounts have not been kept with strict regu-
larity, yet that irregularity has been against Mr. Feargus
O'Connor, instead of in his favor; and that it appears by Mr.
Grey's account there is due to Mr. Feargus O'Connor the sum
of £3,298 5s. 3½d., and by Mr. Finlaison's account the sum
of £3,400.

5. That considering the great number of persons interested
in the scheme and the *bonâ fides* with which it appears to have
been carried on, it is the opinion of this committee that powers
might be granted to the parties concerned, if they shall so
desire, to wind up the undertaking and so relieve them from
the penalties to which they may have incautiously subjected
themselves.

In September the House of Commons agreed to the report of the committee, and O'Connor's land plan came to
an end, and with it his ascendancy in the party.   In their
dismay at the collapse of the project and its disastrous effect upon the fortunes of the political movement with which
it was associated, many Chartists blamed O'Connor unduly.
Certainly O'Connor was blameworthy for inducing so many

poor men to venture themselves in such a dubious enterprise by assuring them that failure was impossible. But if O'Connor had been deliberately dishonest, if he had intended the scheme solely as a means to his personal profit, the investigating committee would certainly have so reported. O'Connor was the acknowledged representative of Chartism in the House of Commons and was highly unpopular with the other members both on account of his personal eccentricities and as the leader of a movement, regarded ever since the events of the tenth of April as the embodiment of the revolutionary spirit. The report of the investigating committee may be accepted as a complete vindication of O'Connor's good faith, though certainly not of his good judgment.

While the Chartist movement was thus distracted by factional warfare it was in no position to take advantage of the outbursts of discontent occurring from time to time among the British poor. The events of 1842 had weakened and discredited the Chartists but had not put an end to labor troubles. Throughout 1843 and 1844 there were agrarian outrages in many places, culminating in the so-called " Rebecca " riots in Wales in which rioters, disguised as women, banded together to destroy the toll-gates whose exactions they found burdensome.[1] In the towns conditions were as bad. In the Sheffield metal trades, especially in the saw works, factories were set on fire or attempts were made to blow them up.[2] In Monmouthshire the failure of an iron works employing more than three thousand men resulted in a wide-spread riot.[3] In Northumberland and Durham the coal miners struck for payment by weight as

[1] Engels, *Condition of the Working Class in 1844*, p. 271.
[2] *Ibid.*, p. 220.
[3] *Annual Register*, pt. ii, vol. lxxxv, p. 72.

measured on standard scales, half-yearly contracts, abolition of the fines system, and employment for not less than
four days a week.[1] By March 31, 1844, the striking miners numbered 40,000. The strike lasted five months and it
was put down at last only by evicting striking miners from
the company cottages. But the Chartists were unable to
convert these industrial disturbances into political demonstrations. The trades unions were more inclined to rely
upon their own efforts and hoped less from political agitation.

By 1846, however, the Chartist movement showed signs
of renewed activity. A significant sign of this revival was
the presentation in Parliament, on March 10, 1846, of 249
petitions, bearing some 1,400,000 signatures in the aggre-
gate, praying for the release of Frost, Williams, and Jones,
Chartist leaders condemned for their part in the Monmouth
insurrection of 1839.[2] In 1847 the movement gathered
to itself still greater strength. O'Connor's land plan was
in the heyday of its popularity, renewed industrial depression seemed to threaten harder times than the dark days of
1842, and the unrest in Ireland and the Continent encouraged the Chartist leaders to hope for an English revolution.
In the August elections many Radicals and some Chartists
stood for the House of Commons. Of the twenty-six
candidates mentioned by Gammage as in sympathy with
the principles of the Charter ten were returned: Duncombe
and Wakley for Finsbury, Sharman Crawford for Rochdale, Muntz and Scholefield for Birmingham, Dr. Bowring
for Bolton, Col. Thompson for Bradford, George Thompson for Tower Hamlets, John Williams for Macclesfield,
and, the greatest triumph of all, Feargus O'Connor for

---

[1] Engels, *op. cit.*, p. 253.

[2] *Hansard*, 3d series, vol. lxxxiv, p. 867.

Nottingham.[1] Most of the candidates supported by the Chartists were not themselves members of the party, but were Radicals who favored political democracy; in O'Connor, however, the Chartists had secured as a spokesman in the House of Commons a man who was not only a Chartist without other party affiliations, but the most prominent of their leaders. The election of O'Connor was important also for the reason that he had as an opponent Sir John Cam Hobhouse, a member of the Whig ministry, whom he defeated by 1,257 votes to 893.[2] Greatly encouraged by this victory, the Chartists proceeded to plan a new petition, much greater than those which the House of Commons had previously rejected, and support it by mass meetings, processions and general agitation. They also resolved upon another convention of the party to determine what steps should be taken in the event of a rejection of the petition by Parliament.

Throughout the winter of 1847-8 the evidences of discontent increased. When the news of the Paris revolt reached England at the end of February the Chartists became at once aggressive. On March 6, 1848, a crowd of some ten thousand persons met at Trafalgar Square in defiance of the orders of the authorities.[3] At the same time trouble occurred in Manchester and elsewhere, notably in Glasgow, where a bread riot resulted in damage to the amount of fifty thousand pounds. Most of the Chartist meetings of this period passed resolutions of sympathy with the French revolutionists and also with the Irish rebels, who saw in the coincidence of bad crops in their own country and the revolutionary outbreaks on the continent an opportunity to

[1] Gammage, *op. cit.*, pp. 283-5.

[2] *Annual Register*, vol. lxxxix, pt. ii, p. 97.

[3] *Ibid.*, vol. xc, pt. ii, pp. 35-7.

rouse the peasantry to a war for Irish independence. A proof of the influence of the French republican movement upon the course of the Chartist agitation in 1848 is furnished by the tone of the Chartist press. Chartist periodicals openly advocated a British republic as the only " thorough remedy " [1] for the evils of the day. No longer content with petitioning for the Charter, they threatened to establish a separate Parliament of " the outlawed seven-eighths " and of " such of the present electors who shall choose to make common cause with the people." [2] They defied the government to use the army to coerce such a popular assembly by means of the army whose " ranks will be filled with Chartists."

At last on the fourth of April the long-heralded Chartist convention met.[3] The moral force section of the party had almost disappeared; O'Connor, O'Brien, Ernest Jones, and G. W. M. Reynolds, the hero of the Trafalgar Square riot, were the most prominent delegates to the convention, and O'Brien resigned on the ninth because he could not approve the violent counsels of the majority. Most of the time of the convention was taken up with speeches by the delegates reciting the poverty existing in the various parts of the country and the determination of those whom they represented not to endure the rejection of another petition. Of forty-seven delegates at least thirty-two reported that their localities were determined upon revolution if this time peaceful measures could not carry the Charter. In case of its rejection, the convention resolved to choose a National Assembly on April twenty-fifth which should sit until the Charter was the law of the land.

[1] J. Barker, *The Reformer's Almanac*, April 15, 1848.

[2] W. J. Linton, *The Republican* (1848), p. 126.

[3] Gammage, *op. cit.*, pp. 301 *et seq.*

Feargus O'Connor claimed 5,700,000 signatures for the Charter, while Ernest Jones estimated the figure at a round six million.[1]   The Chartists planned to carry their petition from a mass meeting on Kennington Common to the Houses of Parliament accompanied by a vast procession of petitioners.   The prospect of a public petition thus formidably supported was enough to alarm conservative sentiment even without Chartist threats of what would follow its rejection. At a meeting on March twenty-seventh, W. J. Vernon, a Chartist speaker, said that " he was for giving the House of Commons only one hour to consider whether they would grant the Charter ", and Ernest Jones exclaimed: " Before heaven, I believe that we stand on the threshold of our rights.   One step, were it even with an iron heel, and they are ours.   I conscientiously believe the people are prepared to claim the Charter.   Then I say—take it; and God defend the right! "[2]

The Chartists openly announced the date of their intended demonstration as the tenth of April.   This publicity gave the government time to take precautions against any seditious uprising which might result from the mass meeting or from the subsequent procession.   The regular army and police were kept as far possible in the background to avoid a possible collision, an army of special constables were sworn in for service on the tenth of April, and the arrangement and management of the forces of law and order were entrusted to the Duke of Wellington.   The government revived for the occasion a long-forgotten statute (the thirteenth of Charles II) directed " against tumults and disorders, upon pretence of preparing or presenting public petitions or other addresses to His Majesty in the Parlia-

[1] Gammage, *op. cit.,* pp. 315-6.
[2] *Ibid.,* p. 299.

ment." [1]   This law, which forbade more than ten individuals
to accompany a petition in person, was revived to prevent
the threatened march on Parliament.   It also prohibited
the signing of any petition by more than twenty persons,
but the government deliberately decided to ignore that part
of the law and to enforce only the section limiting the
number of petitioners who came in person. [2]   The government felt that this statute of Charles II could be only a
makeshift for the occasion, so a bill was introduced on April
seventh, aimed more perhaps at the Irish rebels than at the
Chartists, making certain seditious acts felonies in both
Great Britain and Ireland. [3]   The statute covered the case
of " any person intending to depose the Queen, or proposing
to make war against the Queen, or seeking to intimidate or
overawe both Houses of Parliament, or seeking aid from
any foreign power to invade the United Kingdom with that
intent," and so far was a rather liberal law; for it defined as
" sedition," punishable like other felonies by transportation, many actions that previously had been reckoned as
" treason," punishable by death.   But the act further declared guilty of sedition not only those who plotted rebellion,
foreign invasion or coercion of Parliament, but also all who
might write or " openly or advisedly speak to that effect."
O'Connor for the Chartists and the Irish, and Hume for
the Radicals, led the attack upon this clause, which would,
apparently, make an unguarded political speech punishable
by a long term of imprisonment or transportation.   Their
opposition was fruitless, however, and the bill speedily became law.

On the tenth of April London was garrisoned by some

[1] *Annual Register*, vol. xc, pt. ii, p. 51.

[2] *Hansard*, 3d series, vol. xcviii, p. 95.

[3] *Ibid.*, p. 39.

170,000 special constables, among whom was Louis Napoleon, soon to be President of the French Republic. But the Chartists proceeded to organize their great demonstration as if nothing had happened. The number that gathered on Kennington Common from all parts of the metropolis has been variously estimated from 23,000 [1] to 150,000.[2] Probably the smaller figure is nearer the truth. Contrary to the general expectation, the meeting passed off quietly. O'Connor saw that any form of resistance to the authorities was out of the question under the circumstances and he urged his followers to abandon the projected procession to Parliament. His advice was taken and the procession never was held. The mass meeting quietly dispersed after listening to speeches by O'Connor, Ernest Jones, Julian Harney and other agitators, and the petition was sent to Parliament in three cabs. But the thought of what might have happened if the Chartists had acted up to their bold words remained to disturb the minds of conservative citizens for some time afterwards. The Duke of Wellington, charged with the safety of the city, complained in the House of Lords that even the mass meeting had been permitted:

I do think no great society has ever suffered such a grievance as this metropolis has suffered within the last few days from the error of this great meeting which was to have consisted, it was said, of 200,000 persons. God knows how many thousands really did attend; but still the effect was to place all the inhabitants of the metropolis under alarm, paralyzing all trade and business of every description and driving individuals to seek for safety by arming themselves for the protection of the lives of themselves and of their neighbors, and for the security of their property.[3]

---

[1] *Annual Register*, op. cit., pp. 50-4.

[2] Thomas Frost, *Forty Years Recollections* (London, 1880), p. 139.

[3] *Hansard*, op. cit., p. 71.

The excitement in London was echoed in other parts of the country, and wherever the Chartists threatened violence the authorities forestalled them by elaborate preparation. A striking instance of this was afterwards related by W. H. Chadwick, an influential Chartist:

On the 10th of April . . . thousands of miners were expected to come in the morning to Manchester. When I rose in the morning I found cannon planted all about, and the military parading with drawn swords. I knew that these thousands of men were marching in from Oldham, Rayton, and Shaw, and I at once ran " for my life " by Oldham road, and reached a place called Draylsden Lane. Here I met thousands of men marching in, armed with pikes and other implements of warfare.[1]

Chadwick warned the men of their danger and they dispersed to their homes. Here as elsewhere the dreaded political outbreak failed to materialize. Those Conservative men, who had been so thoroughly alarmed by the prospect of an English revolution paralleling the French, were surprised to find how grossly they had magnified the danger. The violent speeches and vast claims of the physical-force Chartists and the exaggerated apprehensions of their opponents seem alike to have been the result of a false inference from French insurrection to English agitation. When the march on Parliament was abandoned, the men who had feared most from the Chartists became ashamed of their panic and even unduly contemptuous of working class agitation. The monster petition was greeted with shouts of relieved laughter on its arrival in the House of Commons.

On April 13, 1848 the select committee on public petitions made its report to the House of Commons.[2] The

---

[1] Interview in the *Bury Times*, Feb. 24, 1894.

[2] *Hansard, op. cit.*, p. 285.

committee reported that the number of actual signatures to the petition was not over 1,975,496. Of these signatures many were in the same handwriting, and others were obviously fictitious. Queen Victoria, the Duke of Wellington, Colonel Sibthorp (who made in the Commons an earnest but quite needless denial of his part in the matter), and many other persons not hitherto connected with Chartism were listed among the petitioners, together with names sportively invented for the occasion, such as Punch, Pugnose and the like. O'Connor declared that no committee could count the number of signatures on the petition in the short space of time that had elapsed since it was presented, denied all knowledge of the forgeries, and asserted that he could get a Chartist petition signed by many more than he had claimed for this one. The committee replied to O'Connor's attack upon their veracity and related the steps taken to secure a fair count.

There is no reason to doubt that the number of signatures to the Chartist petition was given with approximate correctness by the committee. Joseph Hume on the following February gave the slightly higher estimate of 2,018,000 and pointed out that more than nine thousand other petitions, with a total of 290,559 signatures, also prayed for some extension of the franchise.[1] On either estimate the number of petitioners in 1848 was barely three-fifths of the number in 1842, even assuming that the same allowance must be made for fraudulent signatures in both cases. No doubt the number of signatures was more carefully ascertained in 1848 than in the previous year, but even the most conservative papers accepted without serious question the estimated number in 1842,[2] while the claims advanced by

[1] *Hansard*, 3d series, vol. cii, p. 273.
[2] *Cf. supra*, p. 61.

O'Connor and Ernest Jones in 1848 seem to have had no basis whatever except guess-work. The conclusion is irresistible, that six years of agitation had not only won nothing for the Chartist cause, but had left it in a weaker state than before. In 1848, for the first time, the fact of their declining strength was brought home to the mass of the Chartists.

The force of the reaction from the fiasco of the tenth of April appeared in the elections to the National Assembly. O'Connor opposed its meeting, but his prestige had been greatly damaged among the physical force men by his advice to his followers to abandon their projected march to Parliament, while the moral force men had years before rejected his authority. On May 1, 1848 the new National Assembly met, but the majority of its members were of the moral force faction, and all were conscious of the weakness of their position.[1]   The Assembly chose a new executive, consisting of Ernest Jones, McDouall, McCrae, Kydd and Leach, but could not agree upon any definite course of action to secure the passage of the Charter in Parliament. Neither O'Connor nor O'Brien, the leaders in the party convention of April, were chosen to the Assembly. On the thirteenth it adjourned without accomplishing anything of importance. The secretary of the new executive reported in June that funds were lacking to carry on the work of the party.[2] During the summer O'Connor was discredited yet further by the failure of his land plan, and Ernest Jones became the virtual leader of the movement for the remaining years of its existence.

The political crisis of 1848 ended in the usual repressive measures and trials for sedition. In May there were riots

---

[1] Gammage, *op. cit.*, pp. 324-30.

[2] *Northern Star*, June 15, 1848, cited in Gammage, p. 336.

in Lancashire and Yorkshire, followed by numerous arrests; eighteen Chartists were arrested in Bradford and sixteen in Bingley.[1] On the third of June Ernest Jones and four other agitators were locked up on a charge of sedition, and a mass meeting was dispersed by several companies of infantry and a body of mounted police.[2] The accused Chartists were sentenced in July to terms of imprisonment of two years or upwards.[3] McDouall, arrested at Ashton in July, also received a two years' sentence, and further arrests were made in Manchester, Greenock, Glasgow, Edinburgh, London and elsewhere.[4] On the fourteenth of August a mob armed with pikes and firearms rose at Ashton and murdered a policeman before it could be put down.[5] In London the police discovered three secret armories prepared by a few revolutionary Chartists.[6] As a result of the trials which followed in September William Cuffey and three of the other leaders were transported for life and fifteen others imprisoned, thirteen of them for over two years. The assizes in Yorkshire, Chester and Liverpool resulted in many further sentences to transportation or imprisonment.[7] By the end of the year 1848 insurrectionary Chartism was finally crushed.

These last riots and disorders had behind them no such force of popular approval as the Monmouthshire insurrection in 1839 or the political strike of 1842. They were the acts of a small minority who preferred open revolt for

[1] Gammage, *op. cit.*, pp. 333-4.

[2] *Annual Register, op. cit.,* p. 80.

[3] *Ibid.,* p. 85.

[4] Gammage, *op. cit.,* pp. 336-8.

[5] *Annual Register, op. cit.,* p. 103.

[6] Gammage, *op. cit.,* pp. 337-41.

[7] *Ibid.,* pp. 342-3.

the very reason that they were too few to effect anything by peaceful agitation. The general public did not take them very seriously. According to the *Annual Register* the sensational conspiracy trials in London " excited the least possible interest in the public." [1]   The more pacific activities of the party were equally fruitless. The distinctive representative of Chartism in Parliament, Feargus O'Connor, seemed completely discouraged by the failure of the two plans upon which he had builded his hopes for himself and for the party, the Land Company and the monster petition. He spoke but rarely and then for the most part on Irish affairs. Worst of all, from the standpoint of consistent Chartists, O'Connor made friendly overtures to the middle-class reformers whom he had spent so many years in opposing. He welcomed Hume's attempt to win the householder franchise [2] and appeared very slow in bringing the Charter to the consideration of the House of Commons in which he sat. " Your old friend Feargus," wrote O'Brien in 1849, " has joined the ranks of the Cobdenites for the Cobden budget, and has already won golden honors from journals that made a by-word of his name up to last week." [3]

On July 3, 1849, O'Connor introduced a motion in favor of the principles of the Charter. His own speech was moderate and was seconded by Joseph Hume and other Radicals, although Lord John Russell and the other representatives of the Whigs and the Conservatives who took part in the debate strongly opposed the motion. It was voted down by a majority of 224 to 15; those who supported it were J. Hume, W. J. Fox, J. Greene, L. Heyworth, C. Lushington, Lord Nugent, J. O.'Connell, C. Pearson,

---

[1] *Annual Register, op. cit.,* pp. 121-2.

[2] Gammage, *op. cit.,* p. 349.

[3] *Power of the Pence,* Jan. 27, 1849.

W. Scholefield, H. W. Tancred, Col. Thompson, G. Thompson, Sir. J. Walmsley and the tellers, Feargus O'Connor and W. Sharman Crawford.[1] The nature of the vote shows that all the years of Chartist agitation had made no impression upon the House of Commons, but the number who attended the debate and voted against O'Connor's motion shows as well that the issue of manhood suffrage was still a live one. When O'Connor introduced a similar motion a year later (July 11, 1850) the House was counted out as no quorum was in attendance.[2]

During the years that followed, the principles of the Charter lost interest for the Chartists themselves as well as for the members of Parliament. A clear sign of this was the decline of the party press. As early as December 1848 an anonymous writer complained that whereas in the days of the struggle over the Reform Bill of 1832 " the cheap press circulated in many forms, to the tune of many thousand copies weekly," now the democrats of Great Britain were " scarcely able to keep one going." [3] Two months later it was asserted that there was " not a single daily newspaper in Great Britain of democratic principles; and nearly all the papers are worse edited than they were six years ago." [4] On January 3, 1852, the *Northern Star*, since 1837 O'Connor's organ, changed hands, and Messrs. Fleming and McGowan, the new comers, abandoned the Charter.[5] Ernest Jones's ably edited little paper, the *Notes to the People*, vainly tried to fill the place once taken by the *Northern Star* as the official organ of the party. In May it was

---

[1] *Hansard*, 3d series, vol. cvi, p. 1304.

[2] *Ibid.*, vol. cxii, p. 1284.

[3] *Power of the Pence*, Dec. 30, 1848 (the letter is dated December 18th).

[4] *Ibid.*, Feb. 10, 1849.

[5] Gammage, *op. cit.*, p. 380.

succeeded by the *People's Paper*, but Jones was compelled to solicit funds from loyal Chartists to keep his new venture alive, and within three years it went under for the lack of such support.

Under the strain of loss and discouragement, the remnant of active Chartists were unable to keep the party organization intact. Before 1848 Chartists had frequently divided over questions of tactics or leadership or economic principle, but now for the first time responsible leaders suggested an abandonment or modification of the Charter itself. W. J. Linton expressed the thought of many when he urged the abandonment of the movement:

Chartism has gone down in the whirlpool of its own folly. What escapes the wreck? A handful of men clinging yet to a forlorn hope, that a Conference among themselves, or a new Convention, may reëstablish the party: some few believers in the impossible, waiting for Opportunity to come back.[1]

To restore the old enthusiasm Linton proposed that the democrats of Great Britain form " not merely Chartist, but Republican Associations." [2] Many others felt that Chartism was failing through the insufficiency of its program and the timidity of its spirit, and the republicans of the party claimed fresh converts to their belief.[3] G. J. Harney announced in the prospectus of his *Democratic Review,* that its columns would be " open only to men of ' ultra opinions,' and ' extreme principles ' ".[4] But this tendency to go beyond the Charter evident in the political programs of the later Chartist journalists was rather a sign of increased

[1] *The English Republic*, Feb. 22, 1851.
[2] *Ibid.*
[3] *The People* (1849), vol. i, p. 47.
[4] *The Democratic Review*, June, 1849.

weakness than of increased strength, for it indicated that
the movement was falling more and more into the hands of
a small advanced faction.

Leaders who abandoned the organized Chartist movement, disgusted at its inefficiency or unable to work in harmony with its leaders, did not in all cases cease their work
on behalf of the Charter.   In the years immediately following the disastrous demonstration of April 1848, many rival
organizations were created to further the political and economic principles which had hitherto been embodied in
Chartism.   It is significant that these new organizations
usually added to their political demands an explicit program
of social reform.   The first of these was the People's
League, established by William Lovett in May 1848.   The
League declared for the Charter, the reduction of public expenditure, abolition of customs and excise, and a direct and
progressive property tax.[1]   The new society did not pros-
per.   It failed to rally to its cause either the unenfranchised
masses or the middle-class Radicals and it disbanded in
September of the following year.[2]   J. Bronterre O'Brien,
G. W. M. Reynolds and some other Chartists of a more
radical type than the organizers of the People's League,
founded another body, the National Reform League.   The
National Reform League aimed to steer a middle course between the purely political Chartists and the Socialists.
Without claiming that the Charter was an ideal political
program, O'Brien yet favored it because it had received
the support of so many democrats that it would be " mis-
chievous to risk dividing the people by the propounding of
any fresh scheme." [3]   In addition to the Charter, the Na-

[1] Lovett, *Life and Struggles, op. cit.,* p. 335.

[2] *Ibid.,* p. 349.

[3] J. B. O'Brien, *The Rise, Progress and Phases of Human Slavery,*
p. 109.

tional Reform League advocated the gradual nationalization of all the lands and natural resources in the British
Empire with due compensation to owners, national loans to
producers, and a " symbolic " currency based " either on a
corn or a labor standard." [1]   The clearest statement of the
position of the new organization appeared in O'Brien's
periodical *The Social Reformer*:

The Chartists come the nearest to us; but, as Chartists, they
go only for one right out of many, and that the least valuable
of all *to an uninformed people*, viz. the right of voting for
members of Parliament. . . . The Socialists, on the other
hand, by aiming at *more than the rights* of the people, sacrifice
the attainable for the unattainable.[2]

The National Reform League, like the People's League,
failed to take the place which Chartism had filled in the
affections of the people, and in 1850 O'Brien joined the
National Regeneration Society, another organization devoted to social reform.[3]   During the year the party leaders
endeavored to reunite several organizations, The National
Charter Association, the National Reform League, the Social Reform League, the Fraternal Democrats and the
Trades, into one body, but the attempt was a total failure.[4]
With the single exception of the trades unions, which were
wholly non-political in character, all other reform movements of the unenfranchised classes shared the declining
fortunes of Chartism, till in 1853 a radical periodical could
declare that " there is not on the soil of this country any
party, or popular organization, willing and competent to

[1] *The Social Reformer*, Oct. 20, 1849.
[2] *Ibid.*, Oct. 6, 1849; italics as in the original.
[3] Gammage, *op. cit.*, p. 352.
[4] *Ibid.*, pp. 356-8.

continue the struggle for the triumph of pure unsullied democracy." [1]

Feargus O'Connor, discredited by the fiasco of 1848, allowed his lieutenant Ernest Jones to dominate the Chartist movement for the few remaining years of its existence. Ernest Jones never openly quarreled with O'Connor, who had befriended him when in prison, but he attacked the editors of the *Northern Star* and attempted indirectly to undermine what was left of O'Connor's influence. [2] He ruled the party as autocratically as had O'Connor and was equally successful in promoting division within the ranks. While he denounced the men who were leaving the movement to join other reform organizations, he sadly confessed that " the party of true Chartists that remains is too small to turn the tide." [3] Certainly he did but little to increase it. In his *Notes to the People* he attacked unsparingly the middle-class reformers, the trades-unions, the co-operative movement and the admirers of Louis Kossuth, then the favorite of British democrats. [4] Further secession marked every year of his leadership. In 1850 Thomas Clark broke with the party and founded a rival organization, the National Charter League. [5] This brought down upon him the furious denunciation of the party regulars. G. J. Harney deserted the *Northern Star*, with which he had been associated for many years, and devoted many columns of his new organ the *Democratic Review,* to fiery attacks upon Clark and O'Connor, whom he pilloried as the twin traitors who had tried to wreck the movement. [6] But Ernest Jones could

---

[1] *The Vanguard,* Feb. 12, 1853.

[2] *Cf. infra,* pp. 151-2.

[3] *Notes to the People,* p. 727.

[4] *Cf. infra,* p. 201.

[5] Gammage, *op. cit.,* p. 353.

[6] *Democratic Review,* June, 1850.

not profit by this new attack upon the deserters from the party because he himself had quarreled with Harney.[1]

In spite of daily desertions and intra-party quarrels, Ernest Jones did not despair of the ultimate triumph of Chartism. He believed that if the party were but purged of its weaker members and reorganized on a more efficient plan it would soon recover all and more than all its former strength. He induced the Chartist convention of 1851 to adopt a series of resolutions which amounted to a complete program of social reform of a radically socialistic character.[2] This attempt to inject new life into the moribund movement was rather coldly received. *The English Republic* commented on the efforts of the convention of 1851 : " Your new revival of Chartism . . . must fail for three good and sufficient reasons. 1. You have no party to appeal to. 2. You have no principle round which to form a party. 3. You have no plan of action." [3] The truth of these strictures was so undeniable that Ernest Jones set himself to remodel the party machinery as he had already remodeled the party policies.

Ernest Jones was a member of the party executive in the years 1851 and 1852. At this time, the executive was an unpaid board of nine members, several of whom took very little interest in the work of the party. " I am heartsick," wrote Jones, " of sitting Wednesday after Wednesday with members insufficient to form a quorum; or, when sufficient, doing nothing in the world's greatest and dearest cause . . . I am heartsick of seeing opportunity after opportunity lost because the executive are minding other matters instead of minding the Charter." [4] He advocated as

[1] Gammage, *op. cit.*, pp. 283-5.   [2] *Ibid.*, p. 39.
[3] *The English Republic*, May 22, 1851.
[4] *Notes to the People*, p. 582.

a remedy the reduction of the executive to a well-paid and permanent board of three. In 1852 he withdrew from the executive as a protest against its inefficiency [1] and two of his friends, J. Bezer and J. Shaw followed his example. Of the six members who remained at least four sympathized strongly with the middle-class reformers [2]—which accounts perhaps for their indifference to the Chartist agitation. The next conference, which met in Manchester May 17, 1852, adopted the reorganization plan of Ernest Jones, and he was chosen, together with R. G. Gammage and J. Finlen, on the new executive of three.[3] The decision of the convention of 1851 to stand aloof from all other parties, neither favoring nor opposing them, was confirmed by the program of 1852. The party still resolved:

that since by each and all of the franchise measures now before the people (excepting that embodied in the Charter) the middle-class would gain far more votes than the working-class, which would place the latter in a more powerless position than at present, the Charter must be agitated for in its entirety.[4]

While Ernest Jones labored heroically to keep the Chartist movement from vanishing into a mere vague democratic sentiment, another able Chartist leader was working to the same end. Thomas Cooper, who described himself in 1849 as " a Chartist, though not a member of any Chartist association," [5] took a renewed interest in the affairs of the party after Feargus O'Connor ceased to control it. He urged a new type of tactics, the individual petition, hold-

---

[1] *Notes to the People*, pp. 743-4.
[2] Gammage, *op. cit.*, pp. 384-5.
[3] *Ibid.*, p. 386.
[4] *Notes to the People*, p. 1032.
[5] *Plain Speaker*, June 23, 1849.

ing that monster petitions could never succeed after the failure of 1848.[1] He deplored the growing tendency to accept something less than the full Charter, and protested against " our divisions, as ' Four,' ' Five,' or ' Six Point' men." [2] But he was far from occupying the uncompromising position of Ernest Jones. He divided his time between the Chartist movement and a projected " Progress Union " for general social amelioration, one of the short-lived reform movements so numerous during the latter years of Chartism, and this divided allegiance was of course an offence in the eyes of the orthodox. Moreover, while himself unwilling to work for anything less than manhood suffrage, Cooper did not regard the middle-class reform movement for household suffrage as inimical to the cause of full democracy. " If," he wrote, " a powerful section of the present electors can be brought to unite for the enfranchisement of three and a half millions—and will join with their demand ' the abolition of the Property Qualification'—I wish them success." [3] Such sentiments seemed no less than treasonable to the more class-conscious Chartists, and Ernest Jones refused to allow Cooper to take any share in the work of the Chartist party organization.[4]

Not a few Chartists openly advocated the abandonment of five points of the Charter in order that all democrats in Great Britain might concentrate their efforts upon the most important issue, manhood suffrage, and a distinct manhood suffrage movement was launched in 1852.[5] It was pointed out that the narrow insistence upon each of the six points

---

[1] *Plain Speaker*, June 16, 1849.

[2] *Cooper's Journal*, Jan. 17, 1850.

[3] *Plain Speaker*, June 2, 1849.

[4] Gammage, *op. cit.*, p. 401.

[5] *The English Republic*, Feb. 5, 1852.

had alienated many who were not opposed to a full extension of the suffrage.[1] Many hoped for a revival of the old alliance between the Parliamentary Radicals and the leaders of the working class. A most remarkable expression of this sentiment appeared in 1852 when a working class paper, friendly to Chartism, said: " That the principles of Chartism continue to spread we believe, but little thanks are due to an Ernest Jones and a Feargus O'Connor for it . . . the consummation will be brought about rather by the quiet, moderate and subtle tactics of such leaders as Hume, Cobden, and Walmsley." [2] As might be expected, this editorial expression of opinion called forth several letters of protest from the readers of the paper, but it is at least significant that any Chartist faction should be willing that the democratic movements should be directed wholly by middle-class leaders and wholly by middle-class methods. It is probably safe to say that such an editorial could not have appeared in any working class paper at any time within fifteen or twenty years after the days of the Reform Bill agitation.

The indifference of the country to the attempt of the Chartist organization to recover lost ground was complete. Ernest Jones summarized the political situation well when he wrote in January 1852:

" In the Midland, nothing is doing.
In Scotland—no sign of union.
In the West, an ocean of Democracy, but not a breeze on its surface." [3]

We are fortunate enough to have a barometer of the declining strength of the movement in the number of votes cast at various times for the party executive. In the elec-

---

[1] *The Northern Tribune*, Aug. 20, 1854.

[2] *The Weekly Advertiser and Artizan's Companion*, March 29, 1852.

[3] *Notes to the People*, p. 765.

tions of 1851 the highest of the nine successful candidates received 1,805 votes, the lowest 709.[1] For the year 1852 the corresponding figures were 900 and 336.[2] After the number of the executive had been reduced to three, the leading candidate had 922 votes and the third man 739, or over a thousand less than the candidate third in order of popularity had received three years before.[3] In the last election, for the year 1853, the leading candidate received 942 votes, the third man chosen only 520.[4] This last executive consisted of E. Jones, J. Finlen and J. Shaw, all representatives of the one narrow faction which was the remainder of the great Chartist movement after successive subtractions of the other leaders of the party. The executive was hampered by lack of funds and accomplished nothing. In the year 1854 none was chosen.[5]

Here we may put a period to the history of the Chartist movement, although Ernest Jones, faithful to the end, continued to lecture on behalf of the Charter [6] and did not finally cease his propaganda till 1858.[7] But a leader without followers is not a movement.

[1] Gammage, *op. cit.*, p. 358.
[2] *Ibid.*, p. 380.
[3] *Ibid.*, p. 391.
[4] *Ibid.*, p. 397.
[5] *Ibid.*, p. 401.
[6] E. Jones, *Evenings with the People* (1856-7) ; published lectures.
[7] Schlüter, *Die Chartistenbewegung*, pp. 343-4.

CHAPTER IV

The Improvement in the Condition of the Working Class after 1842

Since the ultimate aim of the Chartist leaders was economic legislation in the interests of the hitherto unrepresented classes, and since it was the economic grievances of the British artisans which provided them with the bulk of their following, it is hard to see how there could have been a real and permanent decline in the movement if the economic condition of England had remained as it was in 1842. Of course the correspondence of Chartist agitation with the varying intensity of poverty can only be traced in the broadest and most general fashion. Our data for the condition of the people during the period of Chartist activity is not only scanty in comparison with the source materials for later decades when the importance of exact and comparable statistics in this field was more fully recognized, but such material as there is was collected for special and immediate purposes. Thus the Parliamentary Reports contain very valuable statements as to the wages of factory hands, miners, hand-loom weavers, and a few other classes of wage-earners at various periods in various places. But it would be hopeless to look in this mass of material for definite annual statements of the trend of wages. The data furnished are the findings of special commissions appointed to investigate the labor conditions of one class of workers at one particular time and, usually, in one particular place or district. For many parts of the country for many years together there may be an absence of source material almost complete; for other times and places the necessary data may be given in a wholly satisfactory form, except for the fact that there is no similar data for other years with which to compare it.

Even if there were the most exact statistics at hand for wages, prices and unemployment for every part of Great Britain and for every month and week of the period under consideration, it would matter little to the present investigation, since there would still be lacking any definite measure of so intangible a thing as a popular agitation. The probable number of signatures to each of the three great petitions furnishes almost all the *statistical* evidence there is of Chartist strength and weakness. The number, activity and circulation of the Chartist periodicals—so far as this can be ascertained,—the votes cast in elections within the organization, the activity of the party at Parliamentary elections, the number of prosecutions for sedition, the estimated size of mass meetings: all such evidence, however useful to confirm a general impression, is of necessity too vague and imperfect to make it possible to establish a mathematical correlation between economic misery and political discontent. It will be enough for our present purpose to ask and answer two questions: was there in the years following 1842 a change for the better in the condition of those classes who furnished the rank and file of the Chartist party sufficiently marked to throw any light on the unexpected weakness of the party in 1848? and was there such a further development in their welfare in the years following 1848 as to explain the impossibility of reviving Chartist agitation after that time, as it had twice been revived after the failures of 1839 and of 1842? If the answer to either of these questions is in the negative, the decline of the Chartist movement must have been due to other than economic causes; if the answer to both is in the affirmative, it is at least highly probable that the chief cause of the decline of Chartism was the partial disappearance of those economic grievances which had made and shaped the movement.

There is abundant evidence that during the years from 1842 to 1846 Great Britain rallied from the hard times which coincided with the greatest strength of Chartism. One measure of this is the real or declared value of the exports of British and Irish produce and manufactures. For the five-year period 1836–40 this value averaged £50,012,994 per annum; for 1841 it was £51,634,623; for 1842, £47,381,023, or less than in any year since 1837.[1] In 1843 export values reached £52,279,709; in 1844, £58,584,292; in 1845, £60,111,082, a total not reached again until 1849. This rapid expansion of trade was accompanied by an equally important development of manufacturing. Leonard Horner, inspector of factories, reported the building of 524 new factories within his jurisdiction from 1842 to 1845.[2] Another indication of recovery was the decline in the number of bankruptcies and insolvencies listed in the *Annual Register*. These increased from 1084 in 1838 to 2120 in 1842. In 1843 there were 1632; in 1844, 1333; in 1845, 1274. The state of the national finances showed a similar improvement. A deficit of nearly four million pounds in 1842[3] was converted into a surplus of £1,443,304 in 1843; of £3,356,105 in 1844, and of £3,817,642 in 1845.[4] The

[1] *Parliamentary Papers*, 1866 (509) lxvi, 717 *et seq.*
[2] Dolléans, *Le Chartisme*, vol. ii, p. 311.
[3] £3,979,539. [4] *Parliamentary Papers*, 1851 (in 140) xxxi, 163 *et seq.*

total national debt, funded and unfunded, declined from £791,757,816 in 1842 to £782,977,684 by 1846; the interest and other annual charges from £29,300,112 to £28,025,253.[1] The language of the royal addresses became increasingly jubilant. As early as August, 1842, the government noted "indications of gradual recovery from that depression which has affected many branches of manufacturing industry";[2] in 1844, an "increased demand for labour";[3] in February, 1845, increased activity in "almost every branch of manufacture" and "a spirit of loyalty and cheerful obedience to the law";[4] in January, 1846, "the prosperous state of the revenue, the increased demand for labour, and the general improvement which has taken place in the internal condition of the country."[5] The value of the testimony of the royal addresses as to the state of the country is, of course, largely negative, indicating little more than the absence of an undeniable depression, but we have confirmatory evidence from the leaders of the opposition. Lord Brougham gave it as his opinion on July 11, 1842, that "the present distress of the country is without a parallel" and that all former hard times "present comparatively an aspect of prosperity."[6] On February 4, 1845, he compared the condition of the country with that of two or three years before; "a contrast more remarkable between the state of the manufacturing classes then and their present condition there cannot be."[7] Lord John Russell admitted in the Commons that there had been "a gratifying improvement in the state of manufactures."[8]

[1] *Parliamentary Papers*, 1857-8 (443) xxxiii, 165 *et seq.*

[2] *Annual Register*, vol. lxxxiv, p. 231.　　[3] *Ibid.*, vol. lxxxvi, p. 3.

[4] *Ibid.*, vol. lxxxvii, p. 2.　　　　　[5] *Ibid.*, vol. lxxxviii, p. 5.

[6] *Hansard*, 3rd series, vol. lxiv, p. 1242.

[7] *Ibid.*, vol. lxxvii, p. 26.　　　　[8] *Ibid.*, p. 74.

We have other evidence of the improved condition of
the people than the increased activity of business and
the surplus in the national treasury. The emigration
from the United Kingdom, which was 128,344 in 1842,
was only 57,212 in 1843.[1] In 1844 and 1845 it was
slightly greater, but it did not reach the old level until
after the Irish famine. The number of marriages to each
hundred thousand of the population increased from 1473
in 1842 to 1515 in 1843; 1597 in 1844, and 1713 in 1845.[2]
The per capita expenditure for poor relief, which
amounted in 1842-3 to 6s. 5¼d., stood at 6s. 0¾d. for
the next two years and fell in 1845-6 as low as 5s. 10½d.,
the rate existing in 1839-40.[3] The percentage of the
population seeking poor relief declined as markedly as
the expenditure for their benefit. In 1842-3, nine and
one-half per cent of the population of England and Wales
received either indoor or outdoor relief from the public
funds; in 1843-4, nine per cent; in 1844-5, eight and
eight-tenths per cent, and in 1845-6 only seven and nine-
tenths per cent.[4] It is not until 1846 that the advance
towards prosperity suffered any check in Great Britain,
although Ireland already suffered in the winter of 1845
from the failure of the potato crop in that year, the first
of a series of bad years in agriculture.

The failure of the potato crop in 1845 and the following seasons only accentuated the dear-food grievance
which threatened a vigorous renewal of both the anti-
Corn Law and the Chartist agitations whenever hard
times should recur. England could no longer feed her-
self. In spite of high protective tariffs the import of

---

[1] Nicholls, *History of the English Poor Law*.

[2] *Parliamentary Papers*, 1847–8 (967) xxv, 1 *et seq.*

[3] *Ibid.*, 1852 (1461) xxiii, 1 *et seq.*

[4] Nicholls, *op. cit.*, p. 390.

grain increased. For the five-year period 1831-35, the per capita annual excess of grain imports over grain exports was 0.036 quarters; from 1836 to 1840, 0.082 quarters; from 1841 to 1845, 0.099 quarters.[1] It is true that the excess importation of wheat and wheat flour, which amounted in 1842 to 2,979,409 quarters, fell to little more than a million quarters for the three succeeding years,[2] but the net importation of other grain and flour increased.[3] In 1842 the average price of wheat per imperial bushel was 7s. 1¾d., distinctly lower than in any previous year since 1837, but higher than in any succeeding year till 1847.[4]

The period from 1846 to 1848 was important in British history for three reasons; there was a partial recrudescence of Chartism,[5] a return of the economic depression which characterized previous periods of political agitation, and a marked change in the attitude of Parliament towards the questions of free trade and factory regulation. The net importation of wheat in 1846 was more than double what it had been in 1845, and the net importation of other grain and meal increased in similar proportion.[6] Prices of grain and meat rose rapidly. In 1845 wheat sold on the average at 6s. 4¼d. per imperial bushel; barley, at 3s. 11½d.; oats at 2s. 9¾d.[7] In 1846,

---

[1] *Parliamentary Papers*, 1867 (88) lxiv, 657 *et seq.*

[2] *Ibid.*, 1843, 1,007,962 quarters; 1844 1,302,828 quarters; 1845, 1,073,-937 quarters.

[3] *Ibid.*, 1842, 550,110 quarters; 1845, 1,184,852 quarters.

[4] *Parliamentary Papers*, 1888 (312) x, 1 *et seq.*, p. 159.

[5] *Cf. supra*, p. 94 *et seq.*

[6] *Parliamentary Papers*, 1867 (86) lxiv, 657 *et seq.*

	Net wheat importation	Net importation of other grain and meal
1845	1,073,937 quarters	1,184,852 quarters
1846	2,202,778 "	2,348,707 "

[7] *Ibid.*, 1888 (312) x, 1 *et seq.*, p. 159.

wheat was at 6s. 1od. ; barley at 4s. 1d. ; oats at 2s. 11½d. In March 1845 eight pounds of beef cost 2s. 8d.; one year later 3s. 8d.[1] During the same year mutton advanced in price from 3s. 4d. to 4s. 4d. The incessant campaign of the Anti-Corn Law League had prepared the public mind for abandoning the time-honored policy of protection to the agricultural interests, and the almost total failure of the potato crop together with a rise in price of grain and of meat gave a practical edge to the theoretical arguments of the League.

From 1842 to 1846 each of the four chief political groups in England had a tariff policy of its own. The Tories favored protection under a sliding scale which would keep prices from rising too high by permitting the importation of grain when it was costly in England, and shutting it out by increasingly high rates of duty when it was too cheap in England to give the farmers a reasonable profit. The members of the party differed widely as to the proper measure of protection to be granted; Sir Robert Peel, as his tariff revision of 1842 showed, [2] favored a moderate scale designed less to secure a monopoly of domestic markets for British farmers than to steady prices against sudden fluctuations such as might result from full competition with foreign growers under free trade. The Whigs, with Lord John Russell as their chief spokesman, were in favor of a fixed duty of a few shillings the quarter—a revenue duty with only incidental protection. The Radicals for the most part favored free trade immediate and complete. The Chartist attitude toward the question was largely negative. While condemning the protectionists,

---

[1] *Parliamentary Papers*, 1851 (in 577) liii, 297 *et seq.*

[2] *Cf. supra*, pp. 65-6.

the Chartists viewed with the greatest suspicion any attempt to deal with the tariff problem by a Parliament which represented only upper-class interests. The gravity of the situation in 1845–6 made Peel a full convert to the necessity for free trade. Against the opposition of a majority of his own party he forced through Parliament a repeal of the whole protective system as applied to agriculture.

The new law placed a duty of ten shillings on wheat when it sold for less than forty-eight shillings the quarter, with a reduction of one shilling duty for each rise in price of equal amount until wheat sold at fifty-three shillings or more, when a duty of four shillings was imposed.[1] This schedule was to hold good only until February 1, 1849, after which time oats, barley, and wheat would pay a nominal duty of a shilling the quarter whatever their price in the British market. Oats in the meantime were to be dutiable according to a sliding scale with a maximum tariff of four shillings the quarter when oats were under eighteen shillings; barley, rye, pease and beans had a maximum duty of five shillings at prices of less than twenty-six shillings. Maize and buckwheat retained only the nominal one shilling duty; duties on animals, meats and vegetables were generally abolished; colonial grain and meal of all sorts sank at once to the rates of 1849. Flour and meal from foreign ports retained duties similar to those on grain; a 196 lb. barrel of wheat-flour, for example, paid the same tariff as 38½ gallons of wheat. The value to the farmers of the small measure of protection retained for three years, was considerably lessened by the action of the government in suspending the Corn and Navigation Laws during the famine; at first

[1] *Hansard*, 3rd series, vol. lxxxiii, pp. 283-4.

till September 1847 ;[1] later till March 1848.[2] But in spite of the measures of the government, food remained at famine prices during 1847, and did not become very cheap until the full force of the new fiscal system was felt in the years following 1849.

The following table has been prepared to illustrate the general trend of the retail prices of foodstuffs during the years 1842 to 1853.[3] In case of each commodity the average for the five years preceding this period (1837–41) has been taken as the base, and the averages for each succeeding year compared with it.

Years	Wheat	Barley	Oats	Beef	Mutton
1837–41 . . .	100	100	100	100	100
1842	89	81	80	91	90
1843	78	87	77	79	82
1844	80	99	86	77	82
1845	79	93	94	87	94
1846	85	96	99	101	107
1847	108	130	120	108	114
1848	78	93	86	106	112
1849	69	81	73	87	94
1850	62	68	69	77	86
1851	60	72	78	75	90
1852	63	84	80	79	92
1853	83	97	88	99	109

The repeal of the Corn Laws in 1846 was but part of a program of liberalizing the British commercial system. Prohibitory and unproductive import duties, export duties and various excises were abolished under the ministry of Sir Robert Peel and afterwards.[4] In 1849

[1] 9 and 10 Vict. c. 1, 2, 3.   [2] 9 and 10 Vic. c. 64, 83.

[3] Compiled from data in *Parliamentary Papers*, 1888 (312) x, 1 *et seq.*; 1851 (in 577) liii, 297 *et seq.*; 1854 (468) lxv, 551 *et seq.*

[4] These changes are particularized in G. R. Porter, *The Progress of the Nation*, revised by F. W. Hirst (London, 1912), pp. 683-4.

the Navigation Laws were repealed,[1] and in 1851 the
vexatious window tax.[2] The total value of export duties,
import duties, excises and other taxes abolished from
1842 to 1850 inclusive amounted to over ten million
pounds.[3] By the end of the period of Chartist agitation
the British tariff was practically one "for revenue only."
The manufacturers and the commercial middle class had
won a complete victory for the free-trade system which
they advocated, but in turn they too were forced to make
concessions. They could no longer resist the demand
for factory reform. The free-trade victory weakened the
opposition to government regulation of the hours of
labor in at least three ways. It deprived the opponents
of state action of their argument that so long as British
industry was hampered by a domestic grain monopoly
British manufacturers could not meet foreign competition
without working their operatives for hours as long as
those which prevailed in other countries. It made un-
tenable the theory, commonly advanced by the Radicals,
that the mere abolition of the Corn Laws would so
improve the condition of the manufacturing interests
that the hours of labor would fall of their own accord to
the level to which philanthropists thought to reduce
them by legislation. Finally, it ranged against the factory
owners the entire political strength of the landholding
classes, who could not see why, if the government abolished the protection which they had so long enjoyed in
order that the laboring population might have cheap
food, it should not also, on similar humanitarian grounds,
grant the factory operatives the reduction in hours which
they desired. The indefatigable earnestness of the factory
reformers, joined to the humanitarianism of the land-

---

[1] By the 12 and 13 Vict. c. 29.   [2] By the 14 and 15 Vict. c. 39.
[3] Detailed in *Parliamentary Papers*, 1851 (in 140) xxxi, 163 *et seq.*

owners (spiced as it was with animosity against the free trade manufacturers), at last prevailed over the opposition of the middle-class element in both of the great political parties and factory reform was accomplished.

But the first important labor legislation during the years of Chartist activity concerned not the textile factories but the mines. The conditions revealed in the investigation of the labor of women and children in mines and collieries so startled Parliament and the nation that Lord Ashley was able to carry in 1842[1] a very drastic law to remedy the evils discovered. The new law absolutely forbade the labor of women and of children under ten years of age below the surface of the ground, provided for the establishing of inspectorships, and instituted certain minor reforms, such as prohibiting the employment of any person under fifteen years of age to take charge of engines or hoisting machinery and forbidding the payment of wages in public houses. Lord Ashley also succeeded in carrying a factory act in 1844[2] which classed women with "young persons," provided for the safeguarding of machinery, lowered the minimum age of employment from nine to eight but enacted a half-time schedule for young children, placed the twelve-hour day for young persons and women between 5.30 a. m. and 8.30 p. m., and increased the power of the factory inspector.[3] But Parliament still refused to grant the fundamental demand of the factory reformers for a ten-hour day for young persons and for women. The principle of regulation, however, was extended in 1845 from the textile factories to the print works.[4]

---

[1] 5 and 6 Vict. c. 99.   [2] 7 and 8 Vict. c. 15.

[3] B. L. Hutchins and A. Harrison, *History of Factory Legislation* (London, 1911), pp. 85-7.

[4] By the 8 and 9 Vict. c. 29.

Lord Ashley's most famous factory bill [1] was introduced in 1846 but postponed for six months on its second reading,[2] and it was not finally carried till 1847. The existing law limited the hours of labor of women and young persons to twelve hours per day; the new bill provided that eleven hours should constitute a day until August 1847—later extended to May 1848,[3] after which time a ten-hour day should be enforced. A way was discovered to evade the provisions of the Act of 1847 by keeping women and young persons at work in "relays," allowing hours of rest between spells of work.[4] Since it was impossible to keep inspectors in every factory at all times to watch over the hours of labor of each individual worker, it was easy for the unscrupulous employer to encroach upon the hours nominally reserved for rest. To remedy this state of affairs, Lord Ashley introduced another bill [5] in 1850 fixing the hours of labor of women and young persons between six in the morning and six at night, or between the hours of seven and seven.[6] Since only one and a half hours were set aside for meal-times, the new day of work was nominally increased to ten and a half hours, but the real protection afforded by the abolition of the relay system was very great. In 1853 similar protection was extended to the labor of children.[7] The importance of this legislation for women and young persons is indicated by the Parliamentary Report of 1850 [8] giving the number of operatives employed in 4330 inspected textile factories :

[1] 9 and 10 Vict. c. 29.

[2] *Hansard*, 3rd series, vol. lxxxv, p. 1080.

[3] *Ibid.*, vol. xci, p. 143.

[4] Hutchins and Harrison, *op. cit.*, pp. 101–3.

[5] 13 and 14 Vict. c. 54.   [6] Hutchins and Harrison, *op. cit.*, p. 105.

[7] By the 16 and 17 Vict. c. 104.

[8] *Parliamentary Papers*, 1850 (745) xlii, 476.

Boys under thirteen years of age.   21,137
Girls under thirteen years of age.   19,638
Male " young persons " from thirteen to eighteen years . . .   67,864
Female " young persons " and women.   329,577
Men over eighteen years of age   157,866
_____
Total number of operatives   596,082

The laboring poor were also the beneficiaries of several mitigations of the New Poor Law of 1834. Many abuses of the system were discussed in Parliament until action was taken to modify its rigors. The apprenticing of pauper children was restricted in 1844,[1] provision was made for their education, and the machinery of administration was improved. By legislation in 1846[2] and 1847[3] persons resident for five years in a parish were secured against removal; in the latter it was determined that married couples over sixty years of age should not be separated in the poor houses,[4] while in 1851 further safeguards were thrown around the interests of pauper apprentices.[5] Thus the three great popular grievances which had done most to build up the Chartist movement, the protective laws which artificially increased the cost of living, the long hours of labor imposed by the factory system, and the severity of the New Poor Law, were acknowledged to be just grievances and were remedied in part during the declining years of Chartism.

In spite of the Corn Law repeal the industrial depression of 1847–8 brought almost as much suffering to the working classes of Great Britain as the preceding crisis of 1842. The distress of the country was so marked as to compel recognition even in the royal address, which stated, in November, 1847, that :

[1] By the 7 and 8 Vict. c. 101.   [2] 9 and 10 Vict. c. 66.
[3] 10 and 11 Vict. c. 110.   [4] By the 10 and 11 Vict. c. 109.
[5] By the 14 and 15 Vict. c. 11.

Her Majesty has seen with great concern the distress which has for some time prevailed among the commercial classes. . . . Her Majesty has deeply sympathized with the sufferings which afflict the labouring classes in the manufacturing districts of Great Britain, and in many parts of Ireland ; and Her Majesty has observed with admiration the patience with which these sufferings have been generally borne.[1]

The finances of the nation showed the effects of the depression very clearly. In 1846 the budget had a surplus of £2,846,308, a decline of almost one million pounds from the surplus of 1845.[2] In 1847 there was a deficit of £2,956,684; in 1848, one of £796,419.[3] The burden of the public debt increased by 1848 to an even greater sum than that of 1842 ;[4] the interest charges, however, were not quite so heavy as during the earlier year.[5] The real or declared value of British and Irish produce and manufactures also decreased, from £60,111,082 in 1845 to £52,849,446 three years later.[6] The number of bankruptcies and insolvencies reported in the *Annual Register* rose from 1274 in 1845 to 2377 in 1848. The poor rate, which was only 5s. 10½d per capita in 1845–6, rose in 1846–7 to 6s. 2½d. and to 7s. 1¾d. in 1847–8.[7] The percentage of the population of England and Wales in receipt of poor relief increased with marked abruptness

---

[1] *Annual Register*, vol. lxxxix, p. 188.

[2] *Parliamentary Papers*, 1851 (in 140) xxxi, 163 *et seq.*

[3] The deficit was due in part to the grants to relieve the agricultural distress prevailing in Ireland. £1,525,000 was appropriated in 1847; £276,377 in 1848.

[4] 1842 £791,757,816; 1848 791,817,338. *Parliamentary Papers*, 1857–8 (443) xxxiii, 165 *et seq.*

[5] 1842 £29,300,112; 1848 £28,307,343. *Ibid.*

[6] *Parliamentary Papers*, 1866 (509) lxvi, 717 *et seq.*

[7] *Ibid.*, 1852 (1461) xxiii, 1.

from 7.9 in 1845–6 to 10.1 in 1846–7 and 10.8 in 1847–8.[1] More was spent in proportion to the population on the relief of the poor in 1847–8 than in any previous year since 1835, but some allowance should perhaps be made for the slightly greater liberality with which the law was administered in 1847 than in 1842.

In most branches of industry no very marked change occurred in the average rates of wages from the early years of Chartist activity to the end of the hard times of 1848. But in most grades of factory labor and manufactures the general tendency was toward improvement. In the cotton factories near Manchester the wages of engine-tenders, stokers, lodge-keepers, warehousemen, reelers, winders, doublers, doffers, all grades of carders, spinners and throstle spinners, showed a substantial increase between 1839 and 1849, the two years selected for comparison in the Parliamentary Report.[2] The hand mule spinners (except the piecers) and the weavers were the only important classes of operatives whose wages declined, or failed to advance. In the woollen mills of Huddersfield and its neighborhood, no grades of labor decreased in price; and of thirty-five grades, twenty-seven showed a distinct advance.[3] On the other hand, the wages of silk weavers, spinners and dyers,[4] and of flax spinners, remained unaltered practically from 1839 to 1849.[5]

The wages of machine workers and metal manufacturers generally showed almost no change from 1839 to 1849,[6] but after 1842 the workers in the iron foundries

[1] Nicholls, *op. cit.*, p. 390.
[2] *Parliamentary Papers*, 1887 (c. 5172) lxxxix, 273 *et seq.* pp. 47–49.
[3] *Ibid.*, p. 95.   [4] *Ibid.*, p. 123.   [5] *Ibid.*, p. 67.
[6] *Wages Report, op. cit.*, p. 171.

made a considerable gain. From 1842 to 1848 the average of the increases for nine grades of labor in the South Wales iron works, was forty-nine per-cent,[1] although a slight decline had taken place in the two years following 1846.[2] The statistics for North Wales, covering the years from 1844 to 1849, show a distinct advance, although here too, as in Staffordshire,[3] the wages level for 1848 and 1849 was lower than for the two preceding years. In the building trades, the average wage increase from 1839 to 1849 was six per-cent[4]; for glass-workers, in the neighborhood of Manchester, fifteen per-cent;[5] in the boot and shoe manufacture, in Worcester and Manchester, seven per-cent.[6] Wages in the potteries remained practically unchanged, although the brick labourers received a slight raise.[7] Of the important classes which furnished the larger number of recruits to the Chartist movement, only a part of the miners and colliers suffered a marked decline in wages between the earlier and the later years of the agitation. The South Wales miners and colliers earned nineteen and a half per-cent less in 1848 than in 1842,[8] but in Staffordshire the average increase in the wages of miners and colliers from 1843[9] to 1848 was nineteen and a half per-cent.[10]

Two other classes of wage-earners remain to be considered : the hand-loom weavers and the agricultural laborers. After 1835 the weekly wages of the hand-loom weavers

---

[1] *Wages Report, op. cit.*, p. 27.

[2] *Ibid.*, p. 31.   [3] *Ibid.*, p. 30.

[4] *Ibid.*, p. 361. Bricklayers, stone-masons, plasterers, slaters, carpenters, plumbers, painters and laborers of Worcester.

[5] *Ibid.*, p. 243. Averages for seven grades of labor.

[6] *Ibid.*, p. 255, p. 258.   [7] *Ibid.*, p. 240.   [8] *Ibid.*, p. 24.

[9] 1842 figures not given for Staffordshire.   [10] *Ibid.*, p. 25.

remained fairly constant at 6s. 3d.,[1] but their numbers
steadily declined. In 1842 there were still some 97,000
hand-loom weavers,[2] a class large enough to count seriously in a political agitation. In 1848 there were only
fifty thousand; and in 1854, at the end of the Chartist
movement, only thirty thousand, or less than a seventh
of the number in the year when the Reform Bill was
carried. R. E. Prothero gives the following estimate of
nominal weekly agricultural wages for 1837 and for
1850–1.[3]

	1837	1850–51
North and North-Western England	12s. 1d.	11s. 10d.
North-East and Eastern England	10s. 4d.	9s. 1d.
South-East England and East Midlands	10s. 0d.	9s. 5d.
South-West England and West Midlands	8s. 10d.	7s. 2d.

It would be a mistake, however, to infer from this table
that the real wages of agricultural labor had declined from
1837 to 1850–1, for prices were much lower in the latter
year than in the former.

In spite of the fall in the wages of agricultural labor in
the years immediately following the repeal of the Corn
Laws, the period of the decline of the Chartist movement was characterized by rapid agricultural development. In the five years from 1840 to 1844 inclusive
only 120,780 acres of land not hitherto under cultivation
were developed, while during the next five years, from
1845 to 1849, 273,967 acres were placed under cultivation.[4] Technical improvement was rapid. The Royal
Agricultural Society, established in 1838, spread scien-

---

[1] G. H. Wood, *History of Wages in the Cotton Trade* (London, 1910),
pp. 127-8.   [2] *Ibid.*

[3] Prothero, *English Farming Past and Present* (London, 1912),
pp. 68-70.

[4] Porter, *Progress of the Nation*, p. 188.

tific knowledge among the farmers. The clay soil was drained at such expense on the part of the landlords and the farmers that in 1846 Parliament appropriated four million pounds to assist in the work.[1] The soil was more carefully manured, and more fertilizer was imported. The importation of Peruvian guano in 1841 was only 1700 tons; in 1847, 220,000 tons.[2] From 1850 onwards steam as a motive power began to be applied in agriculture.[3] But the full return of agricultural prosperity was delayed by low prices and poor crops until after 1853.

The first effects of Corn Law repeal were not of long duration. The average annual net importation of grain and meal was 0.310 quarters per capita from 1846 to 1850; but it decreased to 0.291 from 1851 to 1855.[4] The development of railroading in the fifth and sixth decades of the century was of great advantage to the British farmers in enabling them to transport their crops to market readily and cheaply. By 1854 grain and meat sold for prices as high as those which prevailed under the old protective system, partly because of the abnormal situation created by the Crimean War, partly because of the cheapening of gold which resulted from the opening of new mines in California in 1848 and 1849. The farmers were aided in their attempt to retain the domestic market in competition with the foreign producer by the good years and abundant harvests after 1853.[5] The high degree of agricultural prosperity existing during the decade which followed the end of the Chartist movement was certainly one factor in lessening possible political discontent. The agricultural laborer shared to some degree

---

[1] W. Hasbach, *History of the English Agricultural Laborer*, p. 243.
[2] Prothero, *op. cit.*, p. 366.   [3] *Ibid.*, p. 369.
[4] *Parliamentary Papers*, 1867 (86) lxiv, 657 *et seq.*
[5] Hasbach, *op cit.*, p. 246.

in the new prosperity. From 1850 to 1860 the average
weekly wages for agricultural laborers rose from 11s.
10d. in the northern and north-western counties to 13s.
5d.; in the eastern and north-eastern counties, from 9s,
1d. to 11s. 1d.; in the southeastern and east midland
counties, from 9s. 5d. to 11s. 9d.; in the south-western
and south midland counties, from 7s. 2d. to 9s. 11d.[1]
"So far as the standard of the highest farming is concerned, agriculture has made but little advance since the
'Fifties," wrote R. E. Prothero in 1912;[2] and W. E.
Bear gave as his opinion that, taking everything into
consideration, "the period of ten years ending with 1862
was probably the most prosperous decade ever enjoyed
by British agriculturists."[3]

But Chartism was always an urban rather than a rural
movement, and if hard times had continued in the manufacturing districts the agricultural improvement might
indeed have weakened Chartism but could not have
stopped its progress among the artisans in the towns.
The industrial crisis passed, however, even before the
agricultural depression had come to an end. As early
as February 1849, the royal address congratulated Parliament and the country on the improvement in commercial and industrial conditions,[4] while two years later
the address spoke of "the difficulties felt by that important body among my people who are owners and occupiers
of land."[5] The national finances improved greatly during
the years which followed the depression of 1848. In
place of the deficit existing in 1847 and 1848, there was
a surplus of more than two million pounds in 1849 and

---

[1] Prothero, *op. cit.*, pp. 68–70.   [2] *Ibid.*, p. 346.

[3] H. D. Traill, *Social England*, 6 vols. (London, 1899), vol. vi, p. 409.

[4] *Annual Register*, vol. xci, p. 3.   [5] *Ibid.*, vol. xciii, p. 3.

of over two and a half millions in 1850.[1] From 1848 to
1854 the national debt was diminished from £791,817,338
to £769,082,549; the interest and other annual charges
from £28,307,343 to £27,715,203.[2] In 1848 the real or
declared value of the exports of the manufactures and
produce of the United Kingdom was £52,849,446; in
1853, £98,933,781 ; an increase of more than eighty-seven
per cent in five years.[3] The number of bankruptcies and
insolvencies reported in the *Annual Register* decreased
from 2377 in 1848 to 1009 in 1853.

The clearest evidence of the increasing well-being of
the masses of the people appears in the statistics of
pauperism and criminality. The annual poor rate declined three years later from 7s. 1¾d. per capita in 1848
to 5s. 6½d., the lowest rate since 1838.[4] The percentage of the population of England and Wales in receipt of
poor relief decreased steadily from 10.8 in 1847–8 to 4.8
in 1852–3.[5] The hard times of the early 'forties had
been characterized by much violence and theft. Making
every allowance for the effect on criminal statistics of
the multiplication of laws and their better enforcement,
it seems clear that up to that time criminality had been
on the increase.

In 1841 the number of committals had greatly outstripped the
increase of population in every county in England. In Rutland, which showed the lowest increase of population between
1805–1841, *i. e.*, only thirty per cent., crime had increased 250
per cent. ; in Monmouth, where population had increased

---

[1] 1849 £2,098,126; 1850 £2,578,806. *Parliamentary Papers*, 1851 (in
140) xxxi, 163 *et seq.*

[2] *Parliamentary Papers*, 1857–8 (443) xxxiii, 165 *et seq.*

[3] *Ibid.*, 1866 (509) lxvi, 717 *et seq.*

[4] *Ibid.*, 1852 (1461) xxiii, 1 *et seq.*

[5] Nicholls, *op. cit.*, pp. 390, 424.

most rapidly, *i. e.*, 128 per cent., crime had increased 1720 per cent. . . . For the whole of England, while population increased seventy-nine per cent. between 1805 and 1841, committals increased 482 per cent.[1]

In 1841 the number of committals was 174.6 to each 100,000 persons in England and Wales; in 1851, 156.2.[2]

Much indirect evidence of the prosperity of the period which followed the years of Chartist agitation is contained in the Report of 1865[3] on the improvement in the condition of the people of England and Wales, and the supplementary Report for Scotland and Ireland in 1866.[4] Between the census years of 1831 and 1861 the population of England and Wales increased by 444 per-cent. During the same period the number of day scholars increased by 146.7 per-cent. The amount deposited in savings banks from 1831 to 1864 increased by 209 per-cent, but the number of depositors by 338 per-cent, thus showing that the practice of depositing savings was spreading more and more widely among the masses of the people. Not only the proportion, but the absolute number of paupers decreased from 1849 to 1861, the decrease amounting to 18.8 per cent. From 1839 to 1864 the number of letters delivered by the post office increased in England and Wales by 834 per cent; in Scotland, by 743 per cent; in Ireland, by 556 per cent. Perhaps the most important facts brought out in the first Report dealt with the change in the consumption of certain taxed or dutiable articles of food and drink in the United Kingdom. The use of tea increased 195.36 per cent; the use of coffee, 38.5 per cent; the use

[1] Porter, *op. cit.*, p. 105.   [2] *Ibid.*, p. 110.
[3] *Parliamentary Papers*, 1865 (195) xlvii, 447.
[4] *Ibid.*, 1866 (116) lvii, 843.

of sugar, 119.26 per cent; the use of wine, 83.48 per cent; the use of malt, 32 per cent; the use of spirits, 0.13 per cent.[1]   In other words the per capita consumption of tea, sugar and wine greatly increased, that of coffee and malt underwent little change, while that of spirits showed a marked decline.

It is questionable if British labor received a proportionate share in the rapidly increasing wealth of the British empire of trade, but there can be no doubt that the general rise in wages from the Reform Bill of 1832 to the Reform Bill of 1867 was great enough to revolutionize the daily life of the laborer.   Arthur L. Bowley estimated the change in average weekly wages during this period as follows:[2]

	1833	1867
London artizans	28s. 0d.	36s. 0d.
Provincial artizans	22s. 0d.	27s. 0d.
Town laborers	14s. 0d.	20s. 0d.
Agricultural laborers	10s. 6d.	14s. 0d.

Add to this change in nominal wages the effect of free trade upon the cost of living, the shortening of hours of labor by legislative action, the readjustment of taxation, the decrease in pauperism and unemployment, and the conclusion is irresistible that the peculiar economic conditions which created the Chartist movement largely disappeared during the period of middle-class rule and that the renewed agitation for the franchise had behind it other forces and motives than the misery of the people.

But before leaving the large and important subject of the bearing of economic conditions upon the progress and decline of the Chartist movement, it is well to compare the trend of wages in some typical and important

---

[1] The consumption of domestic spirits showed a *decrease* of 7 per cent.

[2] A. L. Bowley, *Wages in the United Kingdom in the Nineteenth Century* (Cambridge, 1900), p. 70.

industry, the cost of living, and the fortunes of the
movement. For this purpose the average annual wages
in the cotton factories has been taken, not only because
of the importance of the industry in itself and the unusually complete wages data we have for it,[1] but also because it furnished so many recruits to the Chartists.
The average of the wages from 1838 to 1841 inclusive
has been chosen as the basis of comparison with rates of
later years. The index of the cost of living has been
taken by averaging the index numbers of the retail prices
of foodstuffs listed on page 108, but weighting wheat as
double because of its general use in bread.

Years	Wages	Prices	Remarks
1837–41 . .	100	100	The first five years of Chartism.
1842	99	87	Unemployment general. / Monster petition for the Charter. / Political strike in August.
1843	96	80	Chartism inactive.
1844	99	84	
1845	104	88	
1846	104	95.5	Famine in Ireland. / Signs of a revival of the movement.
1847	96	115	Chartist movement active. / O'Connor elected to Parliament.
1848	96	92	Chartist demonstration in April. / Movement shown to be declining.
1849	96	79	Numerous desertions from the party.
1850	96	71	
1851	98	72.5	
1852	100	77	Chartists lack funds to support an agitation.
1853	105	93	The Chartist organization disappears.

[1] Wood, *History of Wages in the Cotton Trade*, pp. 127-8.

CHAPTER V

A Discussion of the Cause of the Decline of the Chartist Movement

The one episode in the history of Chartism which is never omitted even from the briefest narratives of English politics in the nineteenth century is the famous demonstration of the tenth of April in 1848. This is but natural, for the extravagant claims and revolutionary language of the Chartist leaders, the general fear of a revolution paralleling that across the Channel, the garrisoning of London with an army of special police constables including in their number the future Emperor of the French, and finally the pitiable inadequacy both of the demonstration and of the petition to fulfil the hopes or fears universally entertained in regard to them, made the incident worth relating for its own sake as well as for its historical significance. The petition of 1848 was in truth of the greatest significance as evidence both of the weakness and of the strength of Chartism, but the disproportionate emphasis usually given it has made it seem the climax of the whole agitation, and has also made the decline of the movement appear simply the natural consequence of the chagrin of the Chartists over their failure and the ridicule which was heaped upon them after the examination of the petition.

No impression could be further from the truth. In the first place, Chartism had twice before put forth its strength, in 1839 and in 1842, and on both occasions the effort resulted only in failure and repression. The movement seemed as dead in 1840 and in 1843 as in 1849; the difference being that after the first failure the agitation revived stronger than ever, after the second it revived more slowly and in a weakened form, while from the third failure it never recovered. No doubt the cumulative effect of three rejections of their petition tended to discourage the weaker members of the party; but if each occasion had revealed an increasing strength among the people, many others would have joined the movement in the hope that Parliament could not much longer disregard the growing impatience of the people for reform. The agitations for the Reform Bill and for the repeal of the Corn Laws had for many years to meet as unwavering an opposition from the government as the agitation for the Charter, but the Radicals and the Anti-Corn Law League only gained fresh strength at each repulse and persisted in their efforts till they attained final victory. It is improbable that the ruling classes could have resisted indefinitely an agitation for manhood suffrage if that had had behind it the *continuous* and active support of the working classes of the country.

The second reason for rejecting the theory that the collapse of the demonstration of 1848 was the cause of the decline of the movement, is that this collapse itself requires explanation. Even if the theory were adequate to account for the subsequent weakness of the movement, it could not explain its declining strength *before* 1848. As measured by the comparative number of signatures to the petitions of 1842 and 1848, Chartism had hardly three-fifths of the strength in the latter year that it had enjoyed in the former.[1] All careful students

---

[1] *Cf. supra*, p. 101.

of Chartist history agree that the movement was never again so strong as it had been in 1842.[1] Whatever may have been the cause which scattered the forces of Chartism, that cause must have been in operation during the period between the two petitions. The view that the failure of 1848 "killed" the movement exaggerates both the strength of the movement in that year and its subsequent weakness. The fiasco of April was but a milestone set midway on the downward course of the agitation from 1843 to 1853. After 1848 the Chartist party dwindled away, rapidly indeed but not abruptly; the very fact that some semblance of organization was retained for five years later, shows that the party could not have perished merely of the ridicule which met it in 1848.

It is no doubt true, however, that Chartism *as a name* was doomed by the many blunders associated with its history. The later phase of Chartist propaganda was subject to the heavy handicap of all the undesirable associations which had accumulated about the party. Like every other political agitation, Chartism made new enemies with each new shift of policy; like a glacier advancing down an Alpine valley it pushed before it an ever-growing "terminal moraine" of opposition till it could advance no further. The prevailing discontent with the party leadership and the chagrin felt at its ludicrous collapse in the hour of its testing, is evidenced by the numerous reform organizations which sprang up after 1848.[2] Nothing fails like failure, and the ill-success

---

[1] Dolléans heads the section of his work, *Le Chartisme*, which covers the period from 1843 to 1848 "Le Déclin." Tildsley writes: "The Chartist movement remained for a few years but with ever-lessening force. It had reached its height in 1842 and thereafter had no further strength of life." *Die Entstehung der Chartistenbewegung*, p. 52.

[2] *Cf. supra*, pp. 106–113.

of the long-continued Chartist propaganda caused many to feel that if the working classes were ever to win their Charter it must be under some other name.

But we are not particularly interested in the fate of the Charter, for that was but one of many possible democratic programs. What really requires explanation is the comparative indifference of the people to democratic propaganda in every form, the strange political apathy which distinguishes the 'fifties from the earlier decades of the nineteenth century. The faults and failures of the Chartist organization afford no reason why some one of the numerous new radical and democratic organizations which claimed to be heirs of the principles of the Charter should not have revived the agitation for the franchise and carried it to victory, freed of the discredited party label and the unworthy party leadership which had frustrated popular aspirations in the past. But no new working class party appeared to take the place of that which had been abandoned. Such radical propaganda as yet remained was carried on, in a rather mild fashion, within the recognized political parties, Liberal and Conservative. The most important demand of the Charter, that of a widened suffrage, was not granted even in part till more than a decade after the disappearance of Chartism; twenty-five years, in fact, after the time of its greatest strength.

No external political factor will serve to explain the decline of Chartism. The growth and decline of the movement was quite independent of the party warfare of Whigs and Tories. Both parties made concessions to the economic wants of the working classes but neither conceded a single point of the Charter. Both Whigs and Tories showed themselves ready to put down Chartist agitation with a strong hand whenever in their opinion it amounted to "sedition." The Radicals, it is true, were favorable towards the Charter and even used what influence they had in Parliament to secure liberal treatment for individual Chartists who had incautiously put themselves in danger of prosecution. But the Radicals never formed a ministry and, even if they had, it is doubtful if this would have served to break up the Chartist party, since the difference on important economic issues between the Radicals and the Chartists was so great and bitter.[1] The effect of the repressive measures taken against the party leaders was also inconsiderable, or at least temporary. When a champion of the Charter was imprisoned he became a "martyr" to the cause and left prison with enhanced prestige and influence. The Chartist agitators did not lack courage and regarded the chance—or rather the very high probability—of prosecution as one of the inevitable drawbacks to a reformer's life so long as the government remained under the reactionary sway of the upper classes. There is no reason why the prosecutions in 1848, vigorous as they were, should have been more lastingly effective than the prosecutions in 1839, 1842 and 1843.

One marked political weakness the party had, however, which robbed it of much influence possessed by other bodies of reformers; the lack of representation in Parliament. From the very nature of the chief demand of the Chartists, the enlargement of the electorate, it followed that their main appeal must be to the unrepresented. Such influence as they could exert upon Parliament had to be indirect; the moral effect of great mass meetings, monster petitions, strikes, speeches, and the party press. The Chartists could sometime elect an individual spokesman, such as O'Connor in 1847, but they never could

[1] *Cf. supra*, Chap. I.

get votes enough to appear in the House of Commons as a party. In order to get a hearing in Parliament for their demands or their grievances they had usually to call upon the support of some friendly Radical, as a man unable to attend a law suit in person might intrust his interests to an attorney. The position of other notable agitations in the the nineteenth century in which pressure from outside Parliament was the main element of success was very different. The reformers of 1832 might never have forced the House of Lords to yield if the country at large had been indifferent to their cause, but it was none the less a great practical advantage to the Whigs to hold a majority in the House of Commons. The Anti-Corn Law League proceeded to arouse the people and influence the government by such methods as the Chartists employed, mass meeting, petitions, and the like ; but they had practically the entire body of Radicals and many of the Whigs as their Parliamentary agents and, in the later years of their propaganda, the growing sympathy of the prime minister himself. The Irish Nationalists in the days of Parnell and afterwards were only a small minority as compared with the whole House of Commons, but they formed a group which was sometimes able to hold the balance of power between the two great political parties into which the British electorate was and is divided. Agrarian disorders made it impossible for England to continue to ignore the grievances of Ireland ; but only when the fate of a ministry depended upon its paying attention to the Irish account of these grievances as presented to it by a small but compact Parliamentary group, were methods of coercion gradually replaced by remedial legislation.

Since the unenfranchised workingmen who made up the bulk of the Chartist party could exert little or no direct influence on the course of legislation, there remained only two possible paths to success. Either they could win to their support men of a different class who were represented in Parliament by convincing them that their demands were just, or at least that it would be unwise not to yield to them, or else they might carry through a revolution in which the authority of Parliament would be wholly set aside or ignored. The latter method was never seriously contemplated by any considerable number of the party; the risk of failure was too great and the possibility of success too remote. Even the physical force Chartists thought rather of intimidating Parliament into passing the Charter than of obtaining the Charter without its assent, while the moral force Chartists believed that they could convert the represented classes to Chartism.

As the complaisance of the upper and middle classes was so important to the success of the Chartists, their strong insistence upon class solidarity worked to their great injury. The working class was strong in numbers but wholly without political power and, in those years of poverty, practically without economic strength. If the Chartists had possessed either the voting power or the available funds of the Anti-Corn Law League, they could have carried on a far more extensive and effective agitation than they did. The presence of a few wealthy men in the movement could have tided it over many periods when the Chartist press could hardly keep alive for want of support and when the officials of the party could not be paid their salaries. But with a few exceptions, of which the most notable was O'Connor, the leaders of the movement were almost as poor as the rank and file. Surely the theory of class consciousness was never put more forcibly than by Ernest Jones:

An amalgamation of classes is impossible where an amalgamation of interests is impossible . . . All beyond that pale are our enemies by the law of nature-unconvertible, (excepting of course individual cases of generous and elevated feeling), and therefore not worth the wasting of a single thought or moment. . . . These two portions of the community must be separated, distinctly, dividedly and openly from each other "*Class Against Class*;" all other mode of proceeding is mere moonshine.[1]

Had the Chartists been possessed of but a single program and a single policy, it is possible that the British working class, in spite of its political and economic weakness, might have been welded into a formidable organization by the very insistence upon class lines that lost Chartism the powerful aid of the middle-class Radicals. But the history of the Chartist movement is a continuous narrative of schisms and heresy trials over matters of economic doctrine, of political policy or simply of personal pique. It is probable that the party at no time had sufficient cohesion to secure its aims even if all other circumstances had favored its success.

The root difficulty was that the aims of the party were really economic rather than political,[2] while its program was purely political. If Chartism had been only a movement for political reform, there would have been no cause for quarrel with middle-class reformers who desired the same thing, there would have been no serious friction over the different economic theories held by the different leaders, and the improvement in the economic condition of the working classes would not have affected the progress of the agitation. The Charter in itself was a very

---

[1] *Notes to the People*, p. 342, capitals in the original.

[2] The economic aims and views of the Chartists are treated in Chapter I.

simple political program and all factions of Chartists adhered to it with a tenacity which left little ground for dispute on the question of the "party platform," while the differences of opinion as to policy and method, serious as they were, were not peculiar to the Chartist movement but common to almost all radical reform movements. But "the Charter" had various meanings to the different persons who used the term. To almost all it meant more than manhood suffrage, vote by ballot and the other four points demanded by the party. It was about *what* more it meant that the leaders differed, and differed irreconcilably.

To William Lovett the Charter was but one element in a general program of social amelioration by voluntary effort and popular education. To Feargus O'Connor it was the political counterpart of a new peasantry reestablished on the land stolen from their forefathers and removed forever from the factory towns. To the Reverend Joseph Stephens, to John Frost and many of the other early leaders Chartism meant the repeal of the New Poor Law. To J. Bronterre O'Brien it meant currency reform and the nationalization of land rents. To Ernest Jones, Chartism was proletarian Socialism. The incessant and bitter intra-party disputes were not the differences of opinion between persons who were agreed as to the end of their efforts but quarreled over the means to attain it, but the fundamental divergences of men whose aims were wide apart and whose only bond of union was agreement upon the Charter as the indispensable means to attain their diverse and conflicting ends.

It was just this lack of a definite economic program corresponding to the political program of the "six points" that made a few individual leaders of such overmastering importance in the movement. Each of the

leaders and important journalists of the Chartist party
had his views of the ultimate aims to which the Charter
was a means and urged them in season and out, till these
policies became indissolubly associated with the personalities of their leading advocates. Chartists did not
group themselves as individualists or collectivists, but as
O'Connorites, O'Brienites, and the like. As has been
frequently pointed out, Chartism was essentially a negative movement, a protest against the rigidity of the
New Poor Law, the abuses of the factory system, the
burden of the public debt, the class character of the
franchise and numerous other popular grievances. For
this reason it swept into its ranks all kinds of discontent
and thus gained enormous strength from the start. But
the resulting organization was of too miscellaneous a
composition and contained too many divergent views
and motives to achieve a working harmony. In a word,
the Chartists could not agree upon an economic program, because there was none which all or even most of
the party could accept, nor could they agree to leave economic programs to one side, because it was in such reforms that they were chiefly interested.

The differences of economic theory, if the most fundamental, were far from being the only issues which rent
the movement. Immediate methods were in question
as well as the ultimate goal. It is true that the distinction between the moral force and the physical force
Chartists was neither so clear nor so important as has
generally been assumed.[1] But the two tendencies, to
persuasion and to coercion, did coexist and in such a
way as to checkmate each other. The moral force
Chartists were continually reproached for the acts and

[1] Cf. supra, pp. 82-4.

speeches of their allies, so that their arguments lost much of the effect they might have had if the whole party had been likewise committed to moral force methods. The clearest sign of this was the refusal of Joseph Sturge and his group of Complete Suffragists to accept the name of Chartist, tainted in their opinion with the memories of past violence, although they had already declared for every point of the Charter. On the other hand, the presence of so many moral force men within the party ranks effectually prevented a physical force demonstration on any formidable scale. A revolt in which the rebels could not carry with them even the majority of their own party was not very likely to overawe the government of the British Empire. Such partial insurrections and conspiracies as did mark the course of this, on the whole, remarkably orderly movement were suppressed and punished without the slightest difficulty.

Another source of friction within the party was the jealousy between different bodies of Chartists in various parts of the United Kingdom. We have seen how the proposal to organize an independent Scottish party had threatened the harmony of the movement.[1] The locals in England itself were frequently jealous of each other. London and Manchester Chartists alike aspired to have their respective cities reckoned as the headquarters of the propaganda; London because of its size and political importance, Manchester because the strength of the movement was greatest in the northern manufacturing districts of which Manchester was the heart. In 1851, for example, a most bitter campaign was waged between the Manchester Chartist council with the powerful support of the *Northern Star* on the one side, and Ernest Jones and

[1] *Supra*, p. 82.

G. J. Harney on the other, as to whether the coming party convention should be held in Manchester or in London.[1]

Many writers have laid the failure of Chartism to the unwisdom of the leaders of the party and especially of Feargus O'Connor. There is some truth in this view, for none of the leaders, able as many of them were, held at any time the confidence of all the party. William Lovett, the earliest and perhaps the wisest Chartist leader, failed altogether to conciliate the more violent faction which followed O'Connor, and after 1842 he grew discouraged and abandoned active participation in the movement. Thomas Cooper was a man of great energy and sincerity, but he quarreled easily and made as many enemies as friends. J. Bronterre O'Brien and Ernest Jones were probably the most original and intelligent of those who aspired to the party leadership, but both were thorough doctrinaires, inclined to force out of the movement all who opposed their economic views. Among the other prominent men of the party only O'Connor had a sufficiently commanding personality to attract a large personal following among the rank and file of the Chartists. His aristocratic birth, striking presence and fluent if somewhat incoherent oratory, were assets that counted for much in giving him prestige. He had wealth enough to keep his personal organ, the *Northern Star*, in existence during years when other papers were ruined. It finally became the official organ of the Chartist party and the most widely read workingman's paper in the United Kingdom.[2]

---

[1] For the contest over the convention see especially the *Friend of the People* during the winter of 1850-1.

[2] The maximum circulation of the " Northern Star " was 50,000 a week. Gammage, *History of the Chartist Movement*, p. 18.

But in spite of O'Connor's talents and his real enthusiasm for democracy he was almost the worst choice for leader that the Chartists could possibly have made. His mere association with the movement alienated the middle-class Radicals and Parliamentary friends of Chartism, who regarded him as the most dangerous type of demagogue. His Irish birth and affiliations offended many of the more insular Radicals.[1] Even his friends within the party came to regard him as vain, erratic and unstable. The land plan, which more than anything else established his popularity with the workers, drove into opposition most of the other party leaders, including O'Brien and Cooper, who saw the impossibility of the scheme or feared its effect in distracting the energies of the movement from their proper goal. His very confidence in the enterprise he had fathered was so excessive as to wake the suspicion of reflective men. "Although not a practical banker," he wrote, "I make bold to assert that there is not a better, and but few as good, accountants in the Bank of England."[2] When he wrote an article about the principles upon which his scheme was based he characterized it in the following magniloquent fashion: "I have written a treatise as durable as the land."[3] After his election to Parliament he grew more and more erratic, till in 1852 a select committee of the House of Commons reported on his case[4] and he was adjudged mentally irresponsible. How far O'Connor was fully sane during his years of activity within the Chartist party cannot well be determined. but his eccentricities prompt the suspicion that his mental weakness may have come upon him before it was generally known.

[1] For the harmful effect of the Irish influence on Chartism, *cf. infra*, pp. 179–89.

[2] *The Laborer*, vol. i, p. 187.   [3] *Ibid.*, p. 191.

[4] *Hansard*, 3rd series, vol. cxxii, p. 816.

O'Connor's greatest fault as a leader was his jealousy of possible rivals. He quarreled successively with all the other prominent Chartists, accusing them in the *Northern Star* of treason to the party. The fact that he varied his attacks with effusive eulogies and efforts towards reconciliation did not lessen the distrust which those whom he had libeled felt towards him. By 1848 he and his followers, such as Ernest Jones and Julian Harney, stood practically alone in the movement which he had come to dominate. Within the year he had lost the bulk of his most enthusiastic supporters. The physical force Chartists deserted him after he had failed to carry out the projected demonstration of April tenth in the face of the precautions taken by the government; those who had been captivated by his land plan were undeceived by the failure of the National Land Company and the Parliamentary investigation which ended its existence; Ernest Jones and his other lieutenants found him too inactive in the cause and tried to carry on the movement without him.

Much light is thrown upon the internal divisions of Chartism in a novel which Ernest Jones published serially in his *Notes to the People*. This novel, entitled *De Brassier, a Democratic Romance,* covered the history of the Chartist movement under the thin disguise of a change of names and particular events. It illustrated the various policies and personalities, quarrels and factional fights, the conferences, conventions and public demonstrations, conspicuous in Chartist party politics, but from the most violently partizan viewpoint. "De Brassier" was a wealthy aristocrat who entered a democratic movement in some country, the identity of which was concealed but where the political situation bore much likeness to that of England in the 'forties, partly to gratify a demagogic ambition and partly to escape his creditors. He played havoc with the movement by casting suspicion upon the good faith of the really democratic leaders by getting up huge demonstrations which resulted in the arrest of others, while he himself cleverly evaded the consequences of his acts; and even managed to appear as an apostle of reason and moderation by choosing the right time to desert; and by selling his services to the government as a spy. The novel was well written and attracted much comment from other Chartists. Ernest Jones emphatically denied that he was introducing real personalities into the romance, but Gammage has conclusively shown that the speeches and many of the acts of " De Brassier " exactly paralleled those of O'Connor.[1] If " De Brassier " really stood for O'Connor, as seems certain in spite of the author's denial, the caricature of the leader's motives was both crude and unjust. O'Connor was never a government spy and he coveted popularity rather than money. But the novel is none the less an excellent illustration of the factional spirit which continually frustrated the Chartist agitation, not only because it faithfully reproduces in fictional form most of the intra-party quarrels, but also because the very bitterness of the author's pen is an unintended example of that spirit.

The influence of O'Connor upon the Chartist movement was wholly harmful so far as it went, but it may easily be exaggerated. It was difficult while O'Connor still dominated the popular imagination for wiser leaders to carry out their policies, but when the reins of leadership fell from his hands they had once again an opportunity to direct the course of the movement. The

[1] Gammage, *History of the Chartist Movement*, pp. 361-6.

strength and importance of Chartism was never its leadership, but the extent to which it won the support of workingmen who had not previously taken an active part in radical politics. Throughout the century there were always men to lead a radical political movement, but whether they were wise or foolish individually they could accomplish little while they lacked popular support. For a little while, from 1837 to 1842 and, on a diminishing scale, till after 1848, large numbers of the working classes did enter such a movement and made it important and even menacing in spite of the inefficiency of their spokesmen. The leaders needed the movement more than the movement needed them, and it was lack of continued popular support which in the last analysis made Chartist success impossible.

Some have considered that the loss of popular support was a part of the general political reaction which followed the revolutionary efforts of 1848, represented in England by Chartism.[1] It is true that there was such a reaction towards conservatism, or at least away from revolutionary radicalism, in the England of the 'fifties. But it is not clear that cessation of Chartist activity bore any relation to the politics of the Continent. The ruling classes in England may have lost much of their first sympathy for the democratic movement at home and abroad when the new French republic showed signs of becoming socialistic and the countries of central Europe were torn by civil war, but the Chartists did not share this change of sentiment in the slightest degree. On the contrary, they rejoiced over the revolutionary attempts in France, Germany, Hungary, Italy and elsewhere.[2] Nor was the

---

[1] E. D. Jones, *Chartism—A Chapter in English Industrial History*, in the *Wisconsin Academy of Science, Arts and Letters*, vol. xii, pp. 525-6.   [2] *Cf. infra*, pp. 108-204.

English situation at all analogous to that existing on the Continent. Throughout Europe generally the mere utterance of Liberal opinions, however little seditious in form, was penalized. But while the British upper classes acted promptly and ruthlessly enough to suppress insurrectionary Chartism, they did little to check the moral force agitation. A Chartist orator or publicist was at least as free to advocate the six points after 1848 as before that year. The reaction which really affected the Chartist movement was neither popular revulsion from a radicalism which had been carried to excess, as seems to have been the case among the French peasantry of the Second Empire; nor governmental repression, as was certainly the case among the re-established dynasties of Germany and Italy. The reaction from Chartism in England was simply indifference.

Various causes for this indifference have been suggested, but the economic changes which occurred after 1842 seem the most important. Some of the suggested causes are quite beside the point. Justin McCarthy declared of Chartism: "Its fierce and fitful flame went out at last under the influence of the clear, strong and steady light of political reform and education".[1] Such a statement confuses the downfall of insurrectionary Chartism with that of the party as a whole. The Chartist party was neither composed of the most ignorant men in England nor led by them. The intelligent artizans of the industrial towns of Lancashire, the men who founded trades unions, co-operative societies and mutual benefit societies, formed at all times the mass of the party. Many of the leaders such as William Lovett and Thomas Cooper, were self-educated, but they

---

[1] McCarthy, *History of Our Own Times*, vol. i, p. 103.

were well educated. Thomas Cooper, Gerald Massey, and Ernest Jones were poets of unusual talent; J. Bronterre O'Brien was an economist of genuine ability. Such leading Chartists as Holyoke, Linton, Gammage and others, who have recorded tneir memories of the movement, make the narrative literature of the subject highly interesting, O'Connor himself was an educated man and a lawyer. There is nothing in the mere advance of education which could have weakened Chartism; a better educated body of radicals than the Chartists then were, would have worked for fuller political democracy quite as earnestly and perhaps more effectively. As for political reform putting an end to Chartism, the only important reforms which were realized during the course of the movement were of a purely economic character.

If any single cause of the decline of the Chartist movement was more important than others, it was the detaching from the movement the elements which had given it strength. Chartism was essentially a working-class protest against abuses which were created or maintained by upper-class legislation, and, as these abuses were ended or diminished, interest in the movement which was supposed to hold a remedy for them began to flag. After the factory reformers, the opponents of the protective system, the opponents of the New Poor Law and the masses who ascribed their poverty to the operation of the laws against their interests had been more or less satisfied, the only active members of the party who remained were those few who cared for the Charter for its own sake. The demands of the small body of radical reformers who were such on theoretical grounds were then as always ignored by the government. A reform movement, and Chartism was no exception to this generalization, is usually of no importance in practical politics until it has behind it those who are conscious of a concrete grievance as well as of an abstract anomaly.

Both the regulation of the hours of factory labor and the establishing of free trade benefited the working classes in the long run,[1] but it was rather the mere fact of their enactment than their lasting results which produced an immediate effect upon the fortunes of Chartism. The repeal of the Corn Laws came into operation during a year of famine and it was several months before prices fell even to their level of the past. The law which limited the labor of women and young persons to ten hours a day went into effect at a time of industrial depression when the factories were worked on part time, keeping open not more than seven or eight hours a day.[2] But the free-traders and the factory reformers felt that the results which they desired would surely follow the achievement of their policies and so remained satisfied for the time being with what they had accomplished. Had the return of prosperity been unduly delayed, however, new remedies would probably have found supporters and new contingents of reformers would have joined the Chartist ranks.

The victory of the Anti-Corn Law League was a twofold blow for the Chartists. In the first place, it put an end to the dear-food grievance which had contributed much strength to the agitation for the Charter. In the second place, the Chartists had unwisely put themselves in opposition, not indeed to the repeal of the Corn Laws,

[1] In 1859 factory inspector Robert Baker stated that in spite of the great increase in the factory population "all the diseases which were specific to factory labor . . . have as nearly as possible disappeared." J. M. Ludlow and L. Jones, *The Progress of the Working Class*)London, 1867), p. 105.

[2] Hutchins and Harrison, *History of Factory Legislation*, p. 97.

but to the League as an organization. Ludlow and Jones ascribed the destruction of the Chartist party to its hostility towards the League.[1] H. M. Hyndman, writing from the point of view of a Socialist, agreed as to the effect of the conflict between the two competing reform movements, but placed the blame upon different shoulders. "Unquestionably," he wrote, "the anti-Corn Law agitation was one of the great causes of the Chartists to carry any portion of their political programme. It was a red herring trailed across the path of the democracy."[2] In 1854 the *Northern Tribune* sorrowfully confessed that "the Anti-Corn-Law League triumphed against both Government and working-classes : against at least the active portion of the working-classes, the Chartists."[3] Thomas Cooper has testified that it was "a part of Chartist policy, in many towns, to disturb Corn Law Repeal meetings," adding that for his own part he never disturbed such a meeting or suffered his followers to do so either.[4]

The Chartists antagonized not only the Anti-Corn Law League but the whole Whig party, and with equally unfortunate results. So bitter was their opposition to the Whig ministry that in 1841 those Chartists who were fortunate enough to be entitled to vote were urged to do everything in their power to defeat Whig candidates, even at the risk of electing Tories when the victory of a Chartist was out of the question.[5] "To spite the Whigs,"

[1] Ludlow and Jones, *op cit.*, p. 88.

[2] H. M. Hyndman, *The Historical Basis of Socialism in England* (London, 1883), p. 227.

[3] *Northern Tribune*, Jan. 22, 1854.

[4] *Life of Thomas Cooper*, p. 181.

[5] *McDouall's Chartist and Republican Journal*, May 22, 1841; June 19, 1841.

wrote Holyoake, "the Chartists gave their support to the Tories—their hereditary and unchanging enemies."[1]   He advanced proof of how the Chartists had played into the hands of the Tory party :   "Francis Place showed me cheques paid to them to break up Anti-Corn Law meetings, because their cause was defended by Whigs.   I saw the cheques which were sent to Place by Sir John Easthope and other bankers, who had cashed them." But it must not be thought that the antagonism between the Chartists and the Whigs meant that the Chartists had gone over to the Tories or that the Tories had all become democrats.   The occasional support given to Tory candidates at the polls was merely a political manoeuver to embarrass the Whig ministry.   It was not a very creditable alliance, however, and gave their enemies an excellent chance to damage the reputation of the movement with yet unattached radicals, as Gammage pointed out :

A more fatal policy could not possibly have been adopted ; but for it the Whigs might have sunk into everlasting contempt, but this step armed them with a powerful weapon wherewith to fight the Chartists, and the term "Tory Chartist" was adopted in order to load the Chartists with opprobrium, and too well it had its effect.[2]

There is no better illustration of the harm done the Chartist cause by the attitude of its leaders than the case of Francis Place.   He viewed the rise of the Chartist movement with no little sympathy ; in 1838, indeed, he was associated with William Lovett in draughting the

[1] G. J. Holyoake, *Sixty Years of an Agitator's Life*, 2 vols. (London, 1900), vol. i, p. 85.

[2] Gammage, *op. cit.*, p. 193.

Charter for the London Working Men's Association.[1] But he very soon abandoned the agitation in disgust at the way in which it was conducted, and from about 1850 till his death in 1854 he stood aloof from the movement which he might have done so much to help. He preferred to work with the Parliamentary Radicals and thought that the only important good ever likely to come from the Chartist movement would be to stimulate the Radicals to greater exertions on behalf of democracy by the pressure of popular discontent.[2] He laid his finger on one of the greatest weaknesses of Chartism when he wrote in 1841: " They [the Chartists] think they can effect their purpose by taking pains to make enemies, when they should be seeking to make friends."[3] The Chartists, on their part, distrusted Place as much as he did them, principally on account of his advocacy of the New Poor Law of 1834.[4] Any attempt to champion that obnoxious law was an unforgivable sin in the eyes of the majority of Chartists.

It may be objected at this point that even if the victory of the Anti-Corn Law League had robbed Chartism of its free-trader contingent, and the accomplishment of the ten-hour day had satisfied the more urgent demands of the factory reformers, the grievance of those who had sought in Chartism the repeal of the New Poor Law was never met and they might well have remained within the party until their object too was achieved. But while the Elizabethan law has never been restored, the Amendment Act of 1834 was modified by less stringent administration and also by legislative action.[5] The resentment against the new system was, after all, of a temporary character.

[1] Graham Wallas, *Life of Francis Place* (London, 1898), p. 367.
[2] *Ibid.*, p. 369.   [3] *Ibid.*, p. 376.   [4] *Ibid.*, p. 333.
[5] *Cf. supra*, p. 127.

The agitation against the New Poor Law was a large factor in Chartism only during its earliest period, that is from 1837 to 1842, before the working class had accustomed themselves to the altered conditions of poor relief; a new generation which had never experienced the advantages of outdoor relief felt the deprivation less keenly. But the most important factor in weakening the agitation against the New Poor Law was the improved condition of the people. It was during years of business depression, unemployment and consequent pauperism, that the law was most fiercely attacked, for the excellent reason that more persons were affected by its provisions. As pauperism declined, fewer people were concerned over the hardships endured by the paupers.

The most important element of strength in the movement was, not the opposition felt towards any particular piece of upper-class legislation, but the general misery of the people, in which dear food, long hours of labor and a niggardly policy of poor relief were only factors, however important. It was the return of prosperity which did most to satisfy the greatest grievance of the people, their poverty. It is true that the workers ascribed their poverty to political conditions; that was the reason why they were Chartists. But they would not have been content with any legislation which would have left them in such an intolerable condition as prevailed till after 1842; they would have insisted upon taking part in legislation themselves to see if they could not do more to better matters than a Parliament representing only the well-to-do would dare attempt. The ruling classes offered factory reform and free trade as their solution of what Carlyle named "the condition of England problem"; a marked improvement in the life of the people was needed to convince the country that their remedy was sufficiently radical. The Chartists cared for political democracy and social reform; the Chartist leaders cared very much. But the most important issue with the mass of the party was their livelihood. In 1848 a pamphleteer gave his remedy for Chartism:

Cabineteers, feed the Chartists . . . . or let them feed themselves, by giving them work, and ye need not fear them. They are the most hard-working and hard-headed of the community; but if ye wish to touch *their* brains, read no homily, publish no laws, preach no sermons, call no physical force out, —but feed them.[1]

A very interesting question, though rather aside from the purpose of the present study, is that of how much credit the "cabineteers" deserved for the return of prosperity. Most historians have credited it to the adoption of free trade. Molesworth emphasized the beneficial effects of the New Poor Law in reducing the amount of pauperism.[2] Some have considered that the influx of gold from the California mines quieted agitation by raising prices for the farmers and wages for the operatives at the expense of salaried men and bondholders. The Chartists themselves recognized this factor, and one of the leading periodicals expressed the opinion that the increased gold supply would practically repeal Peel's Currency Act of 1819, so that the fundholder and the mortgagee would clamor against being paid in gold instead of for it.[3] The revolution in the means of communication through the rapidly increasing utilization of steam railways was certainly a factor, and an important

[1] T. Styles, *The Coming Era* (London, 1848), p. 9.

[2] Molesworth, *History of England from the Year 1830*, vol. ii, pp. 381-2.

[3] *Power of the Pence*, Jan. 20, 1849.

one, in the increase of national wealth and the consequent
return of prosperity.

Whatever may have been the causes of the improvement in the lot of the working class, the effect is indis-
putable. As times grew harder the workers turned
their attention to politics, subscribed to the *Northern
Star* and other democratic periodicals, attended mass
meetings for which unemployment gave them leisure,
organized in local Chartist societies and projected monster petitions. The *pulsation* of the Chartist movement
is the best evidence of its real nature. An established
political party either maintains itself at a uniform degree
of intensity, excepting perhaps for a gradual increase or
decrease of strength, or else it concentrates its activity
within a brief period before the principal elections. But
a labor agitation will rise from insignificance to overmastering importance within a few weeks following an
important strike or lock-out or a cut in wages. Chartism
bore the latter character, and its strength may be said to
have varied directly with the misery of the people.[1] Almost
equally significant evidence that economic factors determined the strength and weakness of the movement is the
variant strength of Chartism not only from time to time
but from place to place. Rural England was comparatively unaffected by the agitation. Even among the
factory towns themselves there was great difference in
the intensity of Chartist propaganda. Engels claimed
Manchester as the chief center of trades unionism,
Chartism and Socialism because there the working population had become most thoroughly proletarianized.[2] In
Birmingham, he thought, the partial independence of the

---

[1] For the evidence on this head, *cf. supra*, chaps. ii, iii, iv.
[2] Engels, *Condition of the Working Class in 1844*, p. 240.

artisans in the metal-wares trades was responsible for the lack of collectivist sentiment among the masses of the people. "This peculiar midway position of the Birmingham iron-workers is to blame for their having so rarely joined wholly and unreservedly in the English labour movements. Birmingham is a politically radical but not a Chartist town."[1]

The exact correspondence of periods of intense Chartist activity with industrial depression may, however, be said to fail in one particular. There was a slight *lag* between the worst times and the most marked Chartist demonstrations in 1839, in 1848 and possibly in 1842. The hard times of 1839 really dated from the American panic of 1837, and at the time of the Newport raid and the monster petition to Parliament conditions were slightly improved. The winter of 1841–2, rather than the summer of 1842, seems to have been the time of greatest suffering; by August, the time of the political strike, the ministry already saw signs of industrial improvement.[2] In 1847 prices were much higher than in 1848.[3] But these facts, so far from disproving the causal connection between industrial conditions and Chartist activity supply fresh evidence that such connection existed.

A labor agitation, especially on such a scale as the Chartist movement, must have some time to gather head before it reaches its maximum. It was the coming of hard times in 1837 that really created the Chartist movement: that is, gave demands long familiar to radicals such widespread popular support that they acquired

---

[1] Engels, *op. cit.*, p. 199. And yet Birmingham was the favorite meeting place for the conferences and conventions of the Chartist party; probably because of its central location.

[2] *Cf. supra*, p. 118.   [3] *Cf. supra*, p. 123.

political importance.   But several months of propaganda were required to convert the working classes as a whole to Chartism.   The latter end of a period of depression and unemployment is always most apt to be marked by violent speech and action, because the long continuance of hard times eats into the small capital of a workingman and brings him every day nearer to pauperism, even if the depression itself is not getting more acute.   Thus it happened that Chartist demonstrations were most enthusiastically supported at or near the end of the periods of greatest distress.   Moreover, the periods of the greatest Chartist activity were not always the periods when the party was really the strongest.   In 1847 the movement was probably much stronger than in 1848.   At any rate, such is the irresistible conclusion that the student of Chartism draws from a comparison of Chartist success in the elections of 1847, when O'Connor defeated a Whig minister for a seat in the House of Commons, with the fiasco of April in the following year.   The ill-judged revolutionary attempts of a few of the party in 1848 seem to have been a mere flash in the pan provoked by the stimulating examples of rebellious Ireland and revolutionary France.[1]

Another objection which might be urged against the influence of economic conditions upon the fortunes of the Chartist movement is that while wages rose rapidly in most industries after 1842, in many cases they fell back almost to their old figure by 1848.[2]   The buying power

---

[1] The Chartists were never good judges of their own relative strength or of the proper moment to act.   In 1854, after the National Charter Association had ceased to exist, Ernest Jones told an audience that nothing could prevent the Charter from becoming law within a twelve month.   Gammage, *op. cit.*, p. 399.

[2] *Cf. supra*, chap. iv, for estimates of wages and prices in different years.

of wages was certainly much greater between the depression of 1847–8 and the Crimean War than it had been in the early ' forties under protection ; but during the period of depression high prices prevailed, so that the change in real wages from 1842 to 1848 did not exceed the advance in nominal wages. But there was a great difference between the position of the workers in 1842 and in 1848. During the decade from 1839 to 1849 the average number of hours of labor in a week decreased from sixty-nine to sixty in the cotton factories;[1] from sixty-five and a third to sixty in the woollen factories;[2] from sixty-six to sixty in the silk manufacture.[3] Such reductions in labor are the equivalent of a very marked rise in wages, and some surprise was felt that the manufacturers could afford to maintain the old rates of pay after having been compelled, as the direct or indirect result of legislative action, to lessen the hours of labor.

The wages of the hand-loom weavers did not materially alter during the years which followed the rise of Chartism, and the (nominal) wages of the agricultural laborers even declined.[4] But the agricultural laborers never formed a very important section of the Chartists; while if the condition of the hand-loom weavers did not improve, at least their number decreased so rapidly that their wages rate no longer possessed the same significance.[5] With their disappearance as a class, their grievances disappeared as well. The lot of the agricultural laborer improved greatly during the agricultural revival of the ' fifties and in almost all branches of manufacture wages rose rapidly. Even the miners, who had not

---

[1] *Parliamentary Papers*, 1887 (c. 5172) lxxxix, 273 *et seq.*, pp. 47-9.
[2] *Ibid.*, p. 95.   [3] *Ibid.*, p. 123.   [4] *Cf. supra*, p. 131.
[5] *Cf. supra*, p. 131.

shared in the slight general advance in wages of the preceding decade, enjoyed an increase of about fifteen per cent from 1850 to 1860.[1]

The protection given to labor by legislation was greatly extended by the vigorous growth of trade-unionism and of the co-operative movement. As successors of Chartism and heirs to its adherents, these new industrial developments will be considered more fully in the last chapter. Here it will suffice to mention their double influence upon the decline of the Chartist movement. They absorbed the energies which had hitherto gone into the struggle for political reform. What the workers sought, a reasonably high standard of living, could be, it now seemed to them, more readily attained directly in the economic field than by the indirect method of first winning the suffrage and then improving their lot by legislation. In the second place, co-operation and trade-unionism did in some degree fulfill the hopes placed upon them and may have been the chief cause of the new prosperity, or at least of the share which the working classes enjoyed in it.

The passing of a great movement which had for more than a decade engaged almost the entire political activity of the miners, factory operatives, machine-shop men, hand-loom weavers, and the lower ranks of the industrial population generally, is not to be laid to any single cause. The Chartist movement was complex in origin, diversified in character and consequently hard to trace in its disappearance. But the evidence thus far presented seems to make it fairly certain that there were three outstanding causes of the decline of Chartism:

[1]Bowley, *Wages in the United Kingdom in the Nineteenth Century*, appendix.

Among the leaders there was agreement neither upon ultimate aims nor immediate policies. By their intense factionalism and mutual jealousy they lost the useful, perhaps indispensable, sympathy of radicals outside of the party and split the party itself time and again on each new problem that confronted them. If Chartism could have made headway in spite of its internal dissension, it could only have been by developing and maintaining a strength among the people so formidable as to overawe the government and compel at least a partial recognition of their claims.

The movement could not maintain this necessary strength because most of those who joined it did so less for the sake of political democracy in itself than for the removal of particular grievances. The opponents of the Corn Laws were satisfied on that score by the free-trade victory in 1846; the factory reformers were placated by the enactment of the ten-hour day for women and young persons in textile factories and the prohibition of the labor of women and small children in the mines; the opponents of the New Poor Law by slight modifications in the law and a decrease in pauperism; those whose grievances were on the general score of poverty enjoyed in the years which followed the depression of 1842 a slight increase in wages, a reduction of hours of labor, and a decrease in unemployment. All were impressed by the changed attitude of the government towards working-class grievances and desires.

The loss of those who left the Chartist movement because of the complete or partial satisfaction of their grievances might easily have been made up for by fresh recruits from the ranks of the discontented if the depression of 1847–8 had not been followed by a very marked return of prosperity. The improved conditions in town and country in the years following the downfall of Chartism reduced the political activity of the working classes of Great Britain to a lower level than had been known for at least a generation, and prevented the revival of a popular agitation for the principles embodied in the Charter.

CHAPTER VI

THE RESPONSE OF THE RULING CLASSES OF GREAT BRITAIN TO THE CHARTIST MOVEMENT

WITH the disappearance of Chartism the British working classes ceased for a time to contribute leadership to the movement for political democracy. Neither the struggle for political emancipation nor that for economic betterment ceased with the Chartist agitation, but they were no longer so intimately united as they had been within the movement. The franchise was no less desired than before, but Parliamentary Radicals such as John Bright became the spokesmen for the popular wish and the agitation was carried on by the purely political and constitutional methods favored by these leaders. The British workingmen, those at least who had been associated with Chartism, believed that the principles of the Charter would someday be the law of the land and that through the instrumentality of a democratic Parliament they could better their condition to a degree that would be impossible while still unenfranchised. But they were unwilling to postpone the hope of better wages, cheaper food, shorter hours and better working conditions till such time as they controlled the government; they were impatient to try what might be accomplished by the purely economic methods which they were in a position to employ: the organization of labor, co-operative association, the savings bank and the " friendly society," collective bargaining and the strike. This aspect of the labor movement also attracted the sympathy of many who were not themselves workingmen, although the trade unions and other working class organizations remained for the most part under working class control.

The Chartist movement must be reckoned in many ways a failure, but as a demonstration it was a great success. It is true that the alarm which the great mass meetings, the monster petitions and the reckless language of the party press had inspired in conservative breasts gave place to scorn when each new crisis passed and there was no revolution. But the immediate reaction to some particular phase of the movement matters very little. The important fact is that the Chartist agitation, considered as a whole, was a very impressive chapter in history. However badly led and futile in its methods, at least it showed the enfranchised classes in what misery large masses of the British people lived and how deep was their discontent with the social institutions which made their misery possible. As Viscount Ingestre wrote in the preface to *Meliora*, " now we seem to have at last awakened, as from a dream, to the real condition of these, the great majority of our fellow creatures." [1] Even the humiliating collapse of the great demonstration of April tenth 1848, was not received everywhere with derision. One of the volunteer constables who had protected the peace of London on that occasion warned the ruling classes that " the man who sees nothing in Chartism worthy his most serious thought and earnest attention is a more unwise person than any Chartist." [2] Edward Miall, in his tract on *The Suffrage*, which went through

---

[1] *Meliora* (London, 1852-3) vol. i, pp. 11-12. This work consists of two volumes of essays on social problems edited by Viscount Ingestre (Chas. John Shrewsbury). Among the contributors are various members of the nobility and the established clergy, also physicians, administrators, social workers and a few operatives.

[2] *A Letter from One of the Special Constables in London* (1848), p. 21.

more than forty editions from 1841 to 1848,[1] addressed the middle classes as one of themselves, justifying the Chartists in their desertion of their former allies:

We left them before they ever dreamed of leaving us. We asked their aid to carry the Reform Bill, and they generously afforded it. By their means we gained the object which we sought, and having gained it, neglected them. We gave them the poor law; we said nothing of the corn law. We discouraged agitation; we attached ourselves to the Whigs.[2]

Of course the changed attitude of the upper and middle classes of Great Britain towards social problems should not be ascribed wholly to the effect of the Chartist movement; it was rather a response to the whole labor movement of which that agitation was but a phase. Other manifestations of the same unrest, Owenism, republicanism, labor union violence, incessant " turnouts " in the factory towns and rick-burnings in the country, contributed each its share to the expression of popular discontent. Before the demands of the Charter had ever been formulated there was evidence enough that Great Britain did not enjoy social peace. Men were still active in public life who could remember the Luddite machine breakers, the Peterloo massacre, and, in more recent times, the threat of civil war which helped carry the Reform Bill in 1832 and the vast indignation meetings which met all over England to denounce the New Poor Law of 1834. If Chartism was more effective than other agitations in calling attention to popular grievances, it was only because it focussed, as with a burning glass, so many movements into one. It was certainly the most formidable single movement of the working class

---

[1] Edward Miall, *The Suffrage* (1848), reprinted from the *Nonconformist* in 1841), p. 2.

[2] *Ibid.*, p. 3.

that England had yet known and its lesson was not easily forgotten.

That the response of the ruling classes to the labor movement was not wholly due to fear of revolution, but also to a real interest in the welfare of the workers, is shown by the Christian Socialist movement which coincided with the last years of Chartism. The leaders of Christian Socialism had their own quarrel with the existing industrial system and they were prepared to initiate changes as well as to accept them. The direct influence of the Chartist movement upon Christian Socialism, most clearly evident in Charles Kingsley's novel of Chartism, *Alton Locke,* was rather in calling attention to the distresses of the people than in quickening desire to remedy them. It is true that the Christian Socialists had little faith in the Charter as a political program and none at all in the Chartist party as an organization, but they had every sympathy with the spirit that inspired the movement, the resentment of the working classes at a social order that would do nothing for their betterment and the hope of a social reconstruction in which their desires and interests, would be no longer neglected. The Christian Socialists believed that the most hopeful direction in which the friends of labor could employ their energies was to aid and encourage voluntary association among the working classes, so that they might themselves produce and sell the goods they used, without dependence upon factory owner or middleman. The Christian Socialists concentrated their efforts, therefore, upon the cooperative movement, but they did not neglect other lines of effort—support of the trades unions, the removal of legal restrictions upon the savings bank and the friendly society, and the enactment of more rigorous laws to regulate factory labor and safeguard the health of the towns.

No doubt one of the incidental aims of the Christian Socialists was to recapture the labor movement for the Church. The Owenite Socialists were openly anti-clerical and many of the Chartists were quite as much so. This seems to have been due in part to the burden of an established church upon the public revenue at a time when the degree of poverty was so great that all taxation seemed oppression; in part to the teaching of a long succession of radical leaders, such as Robert Owen, who rejected Christianity on philosophical grounds; and, most of all, perhaps, to the intimate alliance between the greater part of the established clergy and the Tory party. Several ministers of religion must be numbered among the leaders of the Chartists, but with very few exceptions they were dissenters. J. R. Stephens, the fiery opponent of the New Poor Law, had been a Wesleyan preacher; Joseph Sturge, leader of the Complete Suffrage party, was a Quaker; Joseph Barker, editor of the Chartist periodical *The People,* had been a Unitarian minister. The non-conformist Chartists were numerous and powerful within the party, and many Chartist periodicals, such as *The Weekly Adviser* and *Artizan's Companion,* devoted much of their space to agitation for the disestablishment of the Church of England. Among the other clerical friends of the movement was Henry Solly, minister of the Presbyterian church at Yeovil, who referred to the Chartist party in 1842 as one of the " great bodies of men, who . . . represent the Christianity . . . of the country." [1] But another element in the party, represented best by Henry Hetherington and his more moderate friend G. J. Holyoake, were as much opposed to nonconformist Christianity as to the Church of England itself. [2]

[1] H. Solly, *What Says Christianity to the Present Distress?* (1842).

[2] *Cf.* G. J. Holyoake, *Life and Character of Henry Hetherington* (London, 1849), *passim.*

The activities of the Christian Socialists can best be traced through the pages of *The Christian Socialist*, edited by J. M. Ludlow in 1850 and 1851. This weekly periodical chronicled the achievements of the Society for Promoting Working Men's Associations, the hearings before the Parliamentary committee on " Investments for the Savings of the Middle and Working Classes," and the attempts made to improve the living and working conditions of the poor. On the religious side, it published the articles of " Parson Lot " (Charles Kingsley), expounding the democratic character of Christian theology, of different parts of the Bible, and of the history and organization of the Christian churches.

It is not easy to give definite dates for the beginning and end of the Christian Socialist movement. A book written in 1839 by T. H. Hudson bore the title *Christian Socialism,* but its aim was solely to confute the anti-Christian socialism of Robert Owen and it contained little of the positive enthusiasm for radical social reform which marked the later movement. Charles Kingsley took an active interest in the events of 1848, but the Society for Promoting Working Men's Associations was not organized till 1850. In 1854 the Society ran out of funds and discontinued its efforts.[1] But the Christian Socialist leaders continued to work as individuals for the co-operative movement, and the impetus given to the movement by their timely championship is felt even today. One of the most important triumphs of the Christian Socialists during the few years of the definitely organized movement was the Industrial and Provident Societies Act of 1852,[2] introduced in the House of Commons by Mr. Slaney and earnestly supported in all its stages by

[1] Arthur V. Woodworth, *Christian Socialism in England* (London. 1903), p. 30. This book contains a useful bibliography on the subject,
[2] 15 and 16 Vict. c. 31.

the Christian Socialists, facilitating the formation of societies by voluntary subscription.

The Christian Socialist leaders befriended the labor
unions as well as the co-operative societies, though with
more reservation. With labor properly organized on associative principles, they hoped that the labor union, with the
inevitable class feeling and class struggle it implied, would
become obsolete. Under existing conditions, however, the
trades union should be supported. Edward Vansittart
Neale, one of the ablest spokesmen of the Christian Socialists, after deploring the necessity for the labor unions added:

But I must at the same time say, that . . . I do believe that
they have been, in the state of society which exists, the only
means in very many cases, by which the workmen could make
a contract with their employers on anything like fair terms,
and exercise over against them that individual liberty for
which the employers profess so much regard.[1]

The Christian Socialists gave very practical evidence of
their sympathy with the labor movement during the strike
of the Amalgamated Society of Engineers in 1852. On
the first day of the year the engineers struck against over-
time and piecework.[2] Their employers not only refused all
attempts to arrange an arbitration of the matters in dispute,
but insisted that since the question was one of their own
property and their own workmen the well-meaning outsiders
who suggested mediation had better not interfere.[3] They
intimated furthermore that in their opinion the trades union
was an intolerable nuisance in the industrial world and for

[1] E. Vansittart Neale, *May I Not Do What I Will with My Own?*
(1852), p. 15.

[2] For the strike see Sidney and Beatrice Webb, *The History of Trade
Unionism* (London, 1911), pp. 196–8.

[3] *Representation of the Case of the Executive Committee of the Central Association of Employers of Operative Engineers* (1852), *passim.*

their part they did not intend to offer employment in the future to any member of a union. This " Representation " stirred the Christian Socialists to indignant action. During the year three separate replies appeared: E. Vansittart Neale's *May I Not Do What I Will with My Own?*, the reverend Charles Kingsley's *Who Are the Friends of Order?*, and J. M. Ludlow's lectures delivered before the Society for Promoting Working Men's Associations, published under the title of *The Master Engineers and their Workmen.* The Christian Socialists did not content themselves with publicly championing the strikers, but attempted to support the strike by subscribing to the union funds. The engineers were forced to give in at last, however, and the aid so freely rendered by the Christian Socialists accomplished nothing unless we count as a gain the prestige the incident won for them among the workingmen of Great Britain.

The Chartists viewed the Christian Socialist movement variously, taking particular interest in the projects for instituting co-operative associations among the working classes. Thomas Cooper welcomed the movement, commending especially the Working Tailors' Association in which Charles Kingsley and F. D. Maurice had been actively interested.[1] Others were more doubtful of the new ventures. The *National Instructor* feared that small voluntary associations could never successfully compete with the existing great concentrations of capital in the hands of the factory owners.[2] Ernest Jones roundly denounced the whole movement as futile and reactionary. He conducted a vigorous controversy in the columns of his personal organ, *Notes to the People,* with both E. Vansittart Neale and

[1] *Cooper's Journal*, Feb. 16, 1850.
[2] *National Instructor*, Oct. 19, 1850.

Charles Kingsley.[1] But few even of those Chartists who
held that voluntary co-operation was a delusive remedy for
the evils of the time cast any doubt upon the good faith of
the Christian Socialists and the sincerity of their efforts to
ameliorate social conditions. This was not only greatly
to the credit of the men who could inspire such confidence,
but it was important as a sign of the times. The earlier
Chartists had held no such charitable views of the Anti-Corn
Law League and of other reform organizations which competed with the Charter for popular favor; the accepted
theory was that such movements were so many deliberate
attempts to distract the attention and misdirect the efforts
of the workers.

The Christian Socialist movement was but one manifestation of the new attitude of the enfranchised classes toward
social reform. Free trade and Factory Acts were perhaps
the most important reforms achieved during the period of
Chartist agitation, but they were by no means all. Friedrich
Engels early noted the change from an attitude in Parliament of determined resistance to popular demands to one of
cautious concessions, and remarked that " the last session
of 1844 was a continuous debate upon subjects affecting the
working-class, the Poor Relief Bill, the Factory Act, the
Masters' and Servants' Act; and Thomas Duncombe, the
representative of the workingmen in the House of Commons, was the great man of the session." [2] In 1847 R. A.
Slaney, then Commissioner for the Health of Towns, urged
that Parliament establish a national board or commission
to study the needs of the working class.[3] Greater interest
was taken in the question of public education, which was

---

[1] *Notes to the People*, vol. i (1851), 470-6; vol. ii (1852), pp. 606-9.

[2] Engels, *Condition of the Working Class in 1844*, p. 17.

[3] R. A. Slaney, *A Plea for the Working Classes* (1847), p. 144 *et seq.*

probably more poorly organized in Great Britain than in any other country of comparable wealth and civilization.[1] From 1839 to 1845, the period of greatest Chartist activity, the evidence of the marriage registers indicates that thirty-three per cent of the adult men and forty-nine per cent of the adult women in England and Wales were unable to write their names.[2] Much was done by private enterprise to better the situation, and by 1850 there were in existence 702 " Mechanics Institutes ", which gave instruction to over a hundred and twenty thousand working men and women.[3]

Many reformers believed that the unfortunate condition of the poor in the great towns could only be remedied by assisting the surplus population either to settle in the country or find homes in a new land. From 1846 to 1854 inclusive the emigration from the United Kingdom amounted to more than two and a half-millions.[4] So many Chartists left England during this period that, as H. M. Hyndman expressed it, the " leaders of the democratic army were left, so to say, without either non-commissioned officers or veteran troops." [5] Much of this was assisted emigration, and there were those who saw in the encouragement given by wealthy Englishmen to the emigration of the poor, an attempted substitute for the social justice which would assure to every Englishman a comfortable home in his own

[1] Joseph Kay, *The Social Condition and the Education of the People in England and Europe*, 2 vols. (1850) contrasts the education of the poor and the prevailing land system in England with the better conditions in some continental countries, Germany in particular.

[2] *Parliamentary Papers*, 1847-8 (967) xxv, 1 *et seq*.

[3] M. Nadaud, *Histoire des Classes ouvrières en Angleterre* (Paris, 1872), p. 207.

[4] Hyndman, *Historical Basis of Socialism in England*, p. 268.

[5] *Ibid*., p. 265.

country. Richard Oastler, the old-fashioned Tory democrat, saw the matter in this light and, in his paper *The
Champion* (1850-1), varied his attacks upon the factory
system and the inadequate law of poor relief with diatribes
against the advocates of emigration. The period of greatest emigration did not, however, much outlast the Chartist
movement. From 1854 to 1860 the emigration from Great
Britain decreased rather steadily from 116,838 to 35,154;
the Irish emigration from 150,209 to 60,835.[1]

The exceptionally heavy Irish emigration after the potato
famine of 1846 was not without its effect upon the labor
movements of Great Britain. In the first place it relieved
the economic pressure of the dense agrarian population in
Ireland upon the United Kingdom. Throughout the 'forties
the standard of living was even lower in Ireland than in
Great Britain, and thousands of Irish peasants left their
country to settle in the slums of Manchester, Liverpool and
other manufacturing towns and commercial ports, where
they could make sure of a job by underbidding British workingmen and thus lowering the general average of British
wages. In the second place emigration broke the intimate
connection between the popular movements in the two countries which was so marked during the Chartist period.
Chartism was a British movement, but Irish laborers
in Great Britain supported it and even supplied it with leaders, such as James Bronterre O'Brien and Feargus O'Connor, who had once contested the leadership of the Irish
party with Daniel O'Connell. The Chartist petition of
1842 advocated the repeal of the legislative union between
Great Britain and Ireland,[2] and the National Assembly of
1848 also passed a resolution endorsing repeal.[3] William

[1] *Parliamentary Papers*, 1868-9, 1, 487, (397).
[2] *English Chartist Circular*, vol. i, p. 158.
[3] Gammage, *History of the Chartist Movement*, p. 328.

Lovett and other Chartists urged the Irish not to trust in O'Connell and his Whig friends, but to join the democracy of Great Britain in a common struggle against the British aristocracy.[1] Many of the Chartist periodicals, notably Joseph Barker's *The People,* devoted a great deal of space to the insurrectionary attempts of John Mitchell and others in the years of disturbance which followed the famine. After the decline of the Chartist movement, however, the agitation for Irish independence was quite independent of contemporary political events in Great Britain, at least till Gladstone decided to add Home Rule to the Liberal platform.

This loss to British democrats of their Irish contingent was not wholly a bad thing for the British labor movement. The *entente* between the Irish Repealers and the Chartists cost the latter the support and sympathy of many who might otherwise have shown sympathy for their cause. At this time the hatred of the Irish for the English, whom they regarded as oppressors, was repaid by a very hearty contempt on the part of the English (the Chartists were an isolated exception) for what they regarded as the untrustworthiness and unfitness for self-government of the Irish race. Even men as well disposed to Chartism as Kingsley and Carlyle believed that the movement could come to no good so long as it was dominated by Irish leaders.[2] Others who had no particular prejudice against the Irish as a people were frightened or disgusted by the agrarian outrages which marked the course of the agitation for repeal. They hoped that the passing of Chartism meant the passing of Irish influence in working class politics, and no longer held aloof from British labor movements.

[1] *The Radical Reformers of England, Scotland and Wales to the Irish People* (no date).

[2] Notice especially Kingsley's attitude toward the Irish Chartists in *Alton Locke.*

With the Chartist movement disappeared the hope of any immediate reconstruction of the political system of Great Britain. But the attitude of the Liberal and Conservative parties toward political reform had by 1848 undergone a marked change. The provisions of the Charter were no longer regarded as outside practical politics, but both parties took them into serious consideration. As it was rather cynically expressed in the *Sozial-Demokratische Bibliothek,* "As Chartism was dead, that is the workingmen no longer pressed as a class for the extension of their political rights, there lay no more danger for the bourgeoisie in the demands of the Charter." [1] The royal address on February 3, 1852, for the first time since the Reform Bill of 1832 promised definite action on the part of the government to modify the electoral system:

It appears to Me that this is a fitting Time for calmly considering whether it may not be advisable to make such Amendments in the Act of the late Reign relating to the Representation of the Commons in Parliament as may be deemed calculated to carry into more complete Effect the Principles upon which that Law is founded.[2]

In accordance with the pledge which he had made, Lord John Russell introduced on February ninth a measure of reform.[3] His bill provided for a five-pound borough franchise, a general forty-shilling-tax franchise for counties and boroughs, in the counties a five-pound copyholder or leaseholder franchise and a twenty-pound occupier franchise. For Scotland the provisions were similar; but there was no change in the Irish county franchise although a five-pound franchise was proposed for Irish boroughs. In March the

[1] *Die Chartistenbewegung in England,* p. 41.

[2] *Hansard,* 3rd series, vol. cxix, p. 6.

[3] *Ibid.,* pp. 252–68.

new measure was postponed for three months [1] and after the defeat of the Russell ministry on a militia bill the project was dropped.

From 1848 onwards John Bright and the other middle-class Radicals agitated for a program of political reform, sometimes nicknamed the " Little Charter," which included household suffrage, the ballot, triennial Parliaments, more equal electoral districts and no property qualifications for membership in the House of Commons.[2]   The Radicals did not, however, obtain sufficient support among the general public to ensure success.   One Chartist periodical laid the public apathy, perhaps with justice, to the rise of new issues which distracted attention from the struggle for the franchise: "At the present moment Chartism has no hold upon public opinion . . . Next to ' Papal Aggression,' and ' the Great Exhibition,' the public mind is occupied with the Co-operative experiments, the revival of Trades' Unions, and the warlike aspect of affairs in Germany." [3]   At any rate, the next attempt to reform the franchise, made in 1854, met with even less favor than the bill of two years earlier.[4] The Radical leaders and Benjamin Disraeli among the Conservatives wished to proceed with it, but Lord John Russell decided to postpone the projected reform until a more favorable time.   He expressed himself, however, as personally a reformer and laid his change of heart to the events of 1848:

I thought . . . that the temper, the moderation, and the good

[1] *Hansard*, 3rd series, vol. cxix, p. 971.

[2] See for example J. Bright and R. J. Richardson, *A New Movement* (1848).

[3] *The Red Republican*, Nov. 23, 1850.

[4] Only eleven petitions were received on the measure and only four of those were favorable. *Hansard*, 3rd series, vol. cxxxii, p. 840.

sense which were shown by the people of this country in 1848, demonstrated . . . that large classes of the people who yet had no votes were fit for the franchise, and that by being brought within the pale of the representation they would confer a benefit upon our institutions.[1]

As a further proof of the good-will of the ministry to the British laboring classes, Viscount Palmerston, then Secretary of State, informed the House of Commons that the three Chartists, Frost, Williams and Jones, implicated in the Monmouth insurrection of 1839, had received a full pardon.[2]

The intrusion of the problems of foreign policy into British political life greatly hampered and delayed the work of the reformers. After the continental revolutions of 1848 and the subsequent wars and repressions, the Chartists themselves devoted most of their attention to events beyond the Channel.[3] This was true in an even greater degree of the middle classes. The picturesque personality of Lord Palmerston, his vigor and adroitness as an orator, and perhaps a slight touch of the demagogue in his make up, won for him the nickname of " the Feargus O'Connor of the middle classes." [4] It would hardly be too much to say that many who counted themselves good Liberals found in the dash and daring of Palmerston's diplomacy a satisfactory substitute for the troublesome labor of political agitation at home. The Crimean War in 1854 and the Sepoy insurrection in 1857 very naturally occupied the attention of Parliament and the public while they lasted, and it was not until after the immediate excitement over these stirring events had ceased that political agitation was again possible. "As re-

---

[1] *Hansard*, 3rd series, vol. cxxxi, p. 307.   [2] *Ibid.*, p. 448.
[3] *Cf. infra*, pp. 199-204.
[4] J. Morley, *Life of Richard Cobden* (London, 1881), p. 568.

gards the subject of Parliamentary Reform," wrote John
Eardley-Wilmot to Lord Brougham in 1857, " it is manifest
that the public mind does not entertain expectation upon it
now in the same degree as it did before the commencement
of the war with Russia." [1]

Nevertheless the year 1858 saw one of the six points of
the Charter at last made law.   In that year the property
qualification for membership in Parliament was abolished,[2]
and it was remarked in both the House of Commons and
the House of Lords that the measure was one which had
been advocated a decade earlier by the Chartists.[3]   The reform of the suffrage which came in 1867 increased the number of voters from 1,352,970 to 2,243,259 (the number in
1870).[4]   The Reform Bill of 1884 added some two million
more voters.[5]   Excepting only a few of the very poor, the
United Kingdom to-day has universal manhood suffrage, although the existence of the plural vote based on the ownership of property in different constituencies acts as an import
ant check upon the democratic character of the suffrage.
Both of the Reform Acts, in 1867 and in 1884, were accompanied by an extensive redistribution of seats, thus
approximating the Chartist demand for equal electoral districts.   The system of vote by ballot was established in
1872.[6]   The demand for annual Parliaments has never been
met, but a concession has been made in that direction by the
enactment of a quinquennial law.[7]   Members of the House
of Commons have received pay for their services since 1911.
Three points of the Charter have been wholly accomplished
and all have received recognition and substantial fulfilment.

[1] John E. Eardley-Wilmot, *A Letter to Lord Brougham* (1857), p. 8.
[2] By the 21 and 22 Vict. c. 26.
[3] *Hansard*, 3rd series, vol. cl, p. 1507 and p. 2089.
[4] Rose, *Rise of Democracy*, p. 179.   [5] *Ibid.*, p. 206.
[6] By the 35 and 36 Vict. c. 33.   [7] 1 and 2 Geo. V. c. 13.

But the Chartist movement might justly have been reckoned a failure if nothing that it aimed to accomplish except the Charter itself had been established in England.   The Charter in its essentials is today part of the British constitution, but this is less important than the triumph of many of the social and economic reforms for which the Chartists chiefly desired it.   Certain phases of Chartism, it is true, have no modern equivalent.   There has never been, for example, any important political group in Great Britain since the disappearance of Chartism with the tendency towards republicanism which characterized that movement.   But the Chartist theories on regulation of industry, on taxation and on the land question, are today in far greater favor among both economists and practical politicians than in their own day.   Systems of national insurance, of old age pensions, of workingmen's compensation, and, in some measure, of wage regulation, have placed British industry on a transformed basis.[1]   The worst of the slums have been cleaned up by public health legislation, and much has been done by the municipalities to solve the housing question.   The absorption of wealth by death duties and a heavily graduated income tax has made a beginning of that redistribution of wealth which the Chartists advocated.   The British land monopoly has not been broken up, but it maintains a precarious existence against an increasing weight of taxation frankly directed to that end.   In Ireland Gladstone established security for the tenant, and even the Conservatives, under the influence of George Wyndham, have done their part to transform the tenant into a freeholder.   In the earlier part of the nineteenth century economists and statesmen agreed that large-scale farming on a capitalistic basis was superior both economically and socially to the peasant pro-

[1] *Cf.* C. H. Hayes, *British Social Politics* (New York, 1913) for a summary of recent social legislation.

prietorship. Today the leading men of both political parties have come around to the Chartist opinion of the value of the small farm, and land policies differ chiefly on the question of how this desirable change should be brought about.

The reconstruction of the Liberal and Conservative parties in the face of the radical movement among the people bears some analogy to the Counter-Reformation of the Catholic Church when confronted by the Protestant Revolt. Nothing was openly yielded to the Chartists simply because of their demand; on the contrary, the leaders of both of the great parties represented in Parliament remained for many years hostile to the Charter and still more so to the working-class organization which agitated for it. But the attitude of mere resistance was abandoned, repression was accompanied by reform and the grievances of the unrepresented received increasing consideration. The economic and political changes demanded by the Chartists were one by one conceded, slowly and inadequately to be sure, but with a certain inevitableness. Lord John Russell, Sir Robert Peel and Lord Palmerston were conservative by instinct, whatever their party affiliations, but their conservatism expressed itself rather in tempering and modifying radical programs than in contesting them. The movement towards social and political reform was, however, greatly hastened by the rise to leadership of Benjamin Disraeli, William Ewart Gladstone and other men in both party organizations who could not only follow public opinion but could lead it as well.

Disraeli, like his contemporaries in statecraft the Emperor Napoleon and Chancellor Bismarck, believed that aristocracy could never be secure until the poor man, too, felt that he had a " stake in the country." Although he stood with the firmest Tories against the Corn Law repeal championed by Sir Robert Peel, he sympathized not a little with the Chartists and shared to the full their contempt for the

Whigs as traitors to the cause of the people which they professed to champion. He knew that so long as the Radicals in the Liberal party were restrained by the large and very wealthy Whig element, a Conservative statesman could outbid them for popular support without losing the support of his own party. He knew also, what no Chartist seems ever to have realized, that the enfranchisement of the British working classes might not necessarily result in a more radical House of Commons. By following the general outlines of policy which he laid down, the Conservative party has been able to maintain its hold upon a large part of the laboring population, especially in London and the seaport towns, —at the cost of accepting political democracy and programs of social reform with their implications and consequences.

Gladstone, unlike Disraeli, started his political career with very little sympathy for the popular unrest which found expression in Chartism. But his successes in free-trade finance brought him into closer touch and sympathy with the Radicals than Disraeli ever experienced. He understood, as Disraeli never did, the Radical attitude (which was also the Chartist) to international politics, its indifference to the ascendancy of Great Britain in the Empire and of the British Empire in the concert of the powers, and its intense preoccupation with the cause of liberal government in all parts of the earth, even where British interests were not directly involved. His gradual conversion to democracy kept even step with that of the Liberal party, which found itself committed by the time of his death to the political policies of the Radicals and to an ambitious program of social legislation without a parallel in the demands of any numerous political party in English history with the single exception of the Chartists. The Socialists and trades unions have succeeded in organizing a labor party which might have played as militantly class conscious a rôle in our times as did the Chartists in the 'forties, had not the Liberal party reduced it to dependence by borrowing extensively from its policies.

CHAPTER VII

THE PERMANENT INFLUENCE OF CHARTISM ON THE BRITISH WORKING CLASS.

THE gradual abandonment of the Chartist movement after 1842 implied no decrease of class consciousness among the workingmen of Great Britain and no relaxation of their effort to better their condition. The undoubted improvement in the conditions of life and labor in the years which followed the industrial depression of 1842 was only a relative improvement after all. It was not so much that the exceptional prosperity of those years weakened the Chartist movement as that the exceptional misery of the preceding period had created the movement and was alone able to maintain it. In many branches of industry wages were still very inadequate, hours of labor excessively long, and abuses of the employer's power, such as the " truck " system or the payment of wages in goods from the company store,[1] widely prevalent. But the further struggle of the British poor against the social conditions which limited and oppressed them was largely transferred from the political to the economic field. This new phase of the labor movement was, however, greatly aided and strengthened by the training in independent action as a class which the British workingman had learned in the Chartist agitation.

We have the testimony of many Chartists as proof of the popular weariness of purely political agitation. In

[1] Prohibited in 1887 by the 50 and 51 Vict. c. 46.

1851 Ernest Jones admitted that "Every year the revolutionary element has become more languid—every year it has sought some more quiescent means of elevation."[1] For his own part, however, Jones wholly deplored this spirit of indifference and believed that he could stir the people again to revolutionary zeal. Other reformers, who believed in the rightfulness of the Charter as fully as Ernest Jones, rather rejoiced that the masses were interesting themselves in matters more directly vital than mere political privileges. "The true solution of the grand social problem of the age," wrote a working-class periodical in 1852, "is the union of Capital and Labour. Until this be effected, mere political and parliamentary reforms will yield a very trifling and unsatisfactory amount of substantial benefit to the masses of the nation."[2] The new spirit is also well illustrated by a radical pamphlet of 1855:

Manhood suffrage must be the cry and watchword; but let the agitation for manhood suffrage be honest and rational— let the people be honestly told from the outset, that the object of universal suffrage is to get honest laws passed upon Land, Credit, Currency and Exchange, that shall rescue the working-classes from the domination of Landlords and rapacious profitmongers.[3]

The chief of the "more quiescent means of elevation" referred to by Ernest Jones were the co-operative movement and trades-unionism. The co-operative movement began with the weavers of Rochdale, who founded a grocery for themselves and their families with only inci-

[1] *Notes to the People*, p. 3.
[2] *The Weekly Adviser and Artizan's Companion*, Feb. 7, 1852.
[3] *National Reform Tract*, no. 5 (1855).

dental sales to the outside public. This enterprise was launched on December 21, 1844, under the association name of the "Equitable Pioneers," and began business on a capital of £28 and with no supplies on hand but flour, butter, sugar and oatmeal.[1] Each member held and paid for four one-pound shares and received five percent interest on his investment ; the remaining profits being divided among purchasers in proportion to the money spent by each.[2] The new enterprise prospered remarkably. In 1850 the Equitable Pioneers added to their grocery department a corn-mill society, in imitation of co-operative mills already existing in Leeds and Halifax,[3] and, in later years, drapery, butchering, shoemaking, clogging and tailoring branches.[4] The number of members in the association increased from the original twenty-eight in 1844 to 680 by 1852 and to 3450 in 1860.[5] The success of the Rochdale experiment stimulated the co-operative movement in other parts of England, particularly during the early 'fifties when the Society for Promoting Working Men's Associations was active. In the summer of 1850 there were only some fifty co-operative associations in existence; within two years there were about 250 with a total membership of 150,-000.[6]

The co-operative movement did not fulfill all the hopes of its founders. Measurably successful in the field of

[1] Geo. J. Holyoake, *History of Co-operation in Rochdale* (1872, seventh edition), pp. 12–13.

[2] *Ibid.*, p. 36.

[3] *Ibid.*, p. 27.   [4] *Ibid.*, p. 32.

[5] G. J. Holyoake, *History of Co-operation in England*, 2 vols. (London, 1879), vol. ii, p. 50.

[6] V. A. Huber. *Uber die co-operativen Arbeiterassociationen in England* (1852), p. 26.

retail trade, the voluntary associations have never become a major factor in manufacture. But, however limited its sphere of usefulness might be, so far as it went the co-operative movement was a real boon to the British workingman. It gave him in many cases cheaper and better food and clothes, in some cases a good investment for his savings, and, in almost all cases, a valuable training in associated effort. A similar example of voluntary collective action was the increase in the number of "friendly societies" and benefit societies. During the two decades following the Reform Bill of 1832, 13,732 such associations were formed with a total of about four million members.[1]

Several of the Rochdale Pioneers were Chartists,[2] and the Chartist party as a whole came in the end to favor the co-operative movement and even to claim that the idea originated with them.[3] But even the more liberal spirited of the party who had not, like Ernest Jones, taken an openly hostile attitude towards the voluntary associations were sorry to witness the disappearance of the old enthusiasm for political rights before more immediately practical concerns and considered that the improvement of the material condition of the workingman was hardly sufficient compensation for the narrowing of his intellectual interests. Thomas Cooper drew a very graphic picture of the difference between the Lancashire operative of the 'forties and the man of the same class in 1872:

In our old Chartist times, it is true, Lancashire working

---

[1] Webb, *History of Trade Unionism*, p. 160.

[2] The proof of this is afforded by the biographical sketches of the founders of the movement given in Holyoake, *History of Co-operation in Rochdale*, part ii, pp. 6-9.

[3] *Ibid.*, p. 4.

men were in rags by thousands; and many of them often lacked food. But their intelligence was demonstrated wherever you went. You would see them in groups discussing the great doctrine of political justice—that every grown-up sane man-ought to have a vote in the election of the men to make the laws by which he was to be governed; or they were in earnest dispute respecting the teachings of Socialism. *Now*, you will see no such groups in Lancashire. But you will hear well-dressed working men talking, as they walk with their hands in their pockets, of " Co-ops " (Co-operative Stores), and their shares in them, or in building societies.[1]

During the later years of Chartist activity there was a considerable revival of trades-unionism, which had been at a rather low ebb during the industrial depression of 1842 and the years immediately preceding.[2] So long as the Chartist leaders could hope to control the unions they viewed their growth with favor and even took an active part in helping it forward. W. P. Roberts, a friend of Feargus O'Connor and legal adviser of his land bank, was for a time solicitor for the Northumberland and Durham Miners' Union and, after 1844, legal adviser of the Miners' Association of Great Britain and Ireland.[3] O'Connor's own periodical, the *Northern Star*, was long the official organ of the National Association of United Trades as well as of the Chartist party.[4] This National Association, founded in 1845, was an ambitious attempt to organize the whole of the British working class into one industrial association as the Chartists had aimed to unite all of that class into one political party. Thomas Duncombe, a Radical member of the House of Commons,

---

[1] *Life of Thomas Cooper*, p. 393.

[2] *Cf. supra*, p. 45.

[3] Webb, *op. cit.*, p. 164.

[4] Schlüter, *Die Chartistenbewegung*, p. 291.

championed in Parliament both the Chartists and the National Association of United Trades. But the hopes founded on the Association were destined to disappointment. A costly and unsuccessful strike of the tin-plate workers at Wolverhampton crippled it,[1] and the panic of 1847 together with the " political excitements of 1848," which distracted the attention of the workers to political issues and thus caused an " apathy which was particularly observable during the year 1849,"[2] completed the destruction. After 1851 the Association ceased to be of any importance.

The failure of the National Association of United Trades put an end to the attempt to centralize many different branches of industry into a single organization and caused the labor leaders to concentrate their attention upon increasing the efficiency of each individual association. The most important organization of the new type was the Amalgamated Society of Engineers, formed in 1850 from the Journeymen Steam-Engine Makers' and Machine Makers' Society and many local unions incorporated with it.[3] By October 1851 the Amalgamated Society numbered 11,000 dues-paying members, and a few weeks later it tested its strength in a great strike.[4] The strike was hardly successful, but it did not permanently hamper the growth of the Society, which doubled its membership during the next ten years.[5] Other trades hastened to copy the example thus

[1] Webb, *op. cit.*, p. 176.

[2] *Report of the Sixth Annual Conference of the National Association of United Trades, 1850.*

[3] Webb, *op cit.*, pp. 186–95.

[4] For the attitude of the Christian Socialists toward the engineers *cf. supra*, pp. 175–6.

[5] Webb, *op. cit.*, p. 208.

set; in fact, it has been claimed that "scarcely a trade exists which did not, between 1852 and 1857, either attempt to imitate the whole constitution of the Amalgamated Engineers, or incorporate one or another of its characteristic features."[1]

In 1853 the Lancashire cotton spinners formed their present association,[2] and in the same year there was a great strike at the Preston cotton mills. At one time as many as 17,000 operatives were out of work[2] and the strike, which began on the first of November in 1853, did not come to an end till the thirteenth of the following April.[3] The estimated cost of the strike to the employers was £165,000; to the strikers and others affected by the stoppage of the cotton mills, £368,250.[4] In the same year (1853) the Kidderminster carpet weavers and the Dowlais iron workers attempted turn-outs with similar lack of success.[5] These strike failures caused a marked reaction against the policy which had led to them and for several years it was an accepted axiom of the labor unions, except perhaps in some of the building trades, that a strike was a disaster to be avoided wherever possible. The trades unions took full advantage of the years of comparative industrial peace which followed the Crimean War to increase their numbers and strengthen their financial resources, with the result that when the next great strikes occurred they were far better able to meet the strain of temporary unemployment. In 1858 the coal miners near Leeds struck against a threatened fifteen per-cent reduction in their wages and succeeded

---

[1] Webb, *op. cit.*, pp. 204-5.

[2] Henry Ashworth, *The Preston Strike* (1854), p. 25.

[3] *Ibid.*, p. 77.

[4] *Ibid.*, p. 76.

[5] Webb, *op. cit.*, p. 206.

in arranging a compromise on the basis of a seven and a half per-cent decrease.[1]   This strike resulted in the formation of a permanent union.   In 1859 and 1860 a great building-trades strike for a nine-hour day was compromised, and as a result two new unions were founded, the London Trades Council and the Amalgamated Society of Carpenters.[2]   The builders' strike was a notable sign of the solidarity of sentiment which had grown up among the different trades, as more than twenty-three thousand pounds were subscribed by other labor organizations to the strikers' fund.

The later development of trade-unionism, which aimed at the separate organization of each craft and ignored political agitation, was unwelcome to the stricter Chartist leaders.   Feargus O'Connor deserted the trade-unionist cause with which he had been so long identified and declared in 1849 that the unions were an obstacle to the winning of the Charter.[3]   Ernest Jones denounced the labor unions as he had the co-operative societies and, indeed, all other attempts to organize the working class on anything less than the national basis.   In 1851 he wrote:

The Trades' Union has been the greatest upholder (unintentionally) of the present system.   It has made working-men uphold it and defend it, by teaching them to believe that their wages could be kept up without a political change.   It has been one of the most anti-democratic institutions of the modern time.[4]

But such protests were of no avail to check the growth

[1] G. Howell, *Labour Legislation, Labour Movements and Labour Leaders* (New York, 1902), pp. 115-6.

[2] Webb, *op. cit.*, pp. 210-13.

[3] Schlüter, *Die Chartistenbewegung*, p. 293.

[4] *Notes to the People*, p. 422.

of trades-unionism. Ernest Jones lost supporters for the charter by his uncompromising stand, and he gained no converts from the unions to make these losses good.

Not only the co-operative associations and the labor unions, but the Socialists also, found the bulk of their recruits in the class of workingmen who had taken part in the Chartist propaganda. Indeed, the Chartist movement itself was largely akin in spirit to the proletarian Socialism of Karl Marx; and, while few of the Chartist leaders except Ernest Jones and Julian Harney accepted the entire Marxian theory and program,[1] there were few elements of "scientific Socialism" which had not been independently worked out by one or another of the Chartists. Friedrich Engels made a careful study of Chartism during his residence in England,[2] and the *Communist Manifesto* (which was given due publicity by the Chartists[3]) recognized in Chartism rather than in Owenite Socialism the true manifestation of the revolutionary spirit of the British proletariat. Herman Schlüter, the Socialist historian of the Chartist movement, contends that Ferdinand Lassalle, the leader of German Socialism, was greatly influenced by his knowledge of Chartism.[4] The influence of the Chartist movement on Socialism in England was probably even greater than its reflex influence upon continental Socialism, but it was not so immediately effective; since nearly a generation elapsed between the close of the Chartist movement and

[1] Schlüter, *op. cit.*, p. 188. In 1869 Engels declared that Jones was the only prominent English politician of his time who wholly and completely understood the Socialist movement. *Ibid.*, p. 345.

[2] *Cf.* Engels, *Condition of the Working Class in England in 1844, passim.*

[3] The text of the *Communist Manifesto* was printed in *The Red Republican*, November 9, 1850.

[4] *Die Chartistenbewegung*, p. 247.

the organization of the Social Democratic Federation in 1881.[1]

A few examples of Chartist theory will serve to show the likeness between certain aspects of the movement and the contemporary Socialism of France and Germany. Ernest Jones stated the Marxian theory of value when he asserted: " Money-capital did not create labor, but labor created money-capital; machinery did not create work, but work created machinery. It therefore follows, that labour is, by its own nature, the sovereign power, and that it owes no allegiance, gratitude or subjection to capital."[2] J. Bronterre O'Brien, an ardent admirer of Robespierre and also of Babœuf (often considered the first leader of proletarian Socialism), published in 1836 a translation of Buonarroti's history of Babœuf's conspiracy, thus for the first time introducing the work to the English-speaking public. He was not wholly a Marxian Socialist but he called himself a " social democrat," and in his book, *The Progress and Phases of Human Slavery*, he did much to popularize the phrase and to develop the concept of " wage-slavery." The Marxian theory of the total abolition of other classes by the victory of the proletariat has never been more lucidly expressed than by G. J. Harney. " As regards the working men swamping other classes, the answer is easy," he declared, "*other classes have no right even to exist.* To prepare the way for the absolute supremacy of the working classes . . . preparatory to the abolition of the system of classes, is the mission of the *Red Republican*."[3] Even

---

[1] The Chartist leaders were not forgotten, however. A volume of *Revolutionary Rhymes and Songs for Socialists* which appeared in 1886 included Ernest Jones's " Song of the Lower Classes."

[2] *Notes to the People*, p. 74.

[3] *The Red Republican*, July 6, 1850. Italics in the original.

Feargus O'Connor, who had insisted that he was "neither Socialist nor communist,"[1] based his land plan on the Marxian principle of the existence of an industrial reserve army.[2] He believed that wages were only kept down by the presence of a large body of the unemployed ready to take the places of dissatisfied workingmen, and that if a sufficient number of operatives could be settled on the land, the employers would be forced to meet the terms of their remaining operatives.

But it would be wrong to make too much of minor points of agreement between Socialist theory and the opinions of a few Chartist leaders, since, as the Chartists never made their economic program definite, it is impossible to tell to what extent the party leaders represented the views of the masses of their followers. Tactics rather than theory was the chief bequest of the Chartists to succeeding generations of British radicals. For a time the workingmen of Great Britain abandoned independent political action and sought to realize their aims within the Liberal and Conservative party organizations; but they never forgot that during the period of the Chartist agitation they had stood alone as a class and made their strength feared even while they were still without political power. The Independent Labour Party is in a sense the present-day representative of the National Charter Association, less because it favors similar political and economic reforms than because it is avowedly the party of a class. The effect of more than a decade of self-reliant political activity in teaching the British artizan to study and think for himself upon the issues of the day, to express his meaning clearly on the

---

[1] *Northern Star*, Oct. 28, 1848.
[2] *Cf.* Tildsley, *Die Entstehung der Chartistenbewegung*, p. 133.

public platform, to practise the technique of parliamentary law, to experience the realities of legislative and
administrative work, must have rendered him a far more
useful citizen when he was finally enfranchised than he
would have been if the suffrage had been conferred upon
him without special effort on his part to obtain it.

Chartism educated the people also in the narrower
sense of the term "education." To many workingmen
the cheap Chartist papers were the first periodicals they
had ever read, or at least regularly bought. It was
through these papers as a medium that they first studied
the world beyond the range of their own experience. The
Chartist press was very frequently their sole text-book
of history, political geography, English literature, economics and political theory. Most of the Chartist periodicals printed a large amount of poetry, general or
propagandist; most of them published notes on events
in foreign countries which were thought to be of interest
to democrats; many, especially of those to which J.
Bronterre O'Brien contributed, chronicled the origins of
democracy in the remote past, recounting the deeds and
projects of the Gracchi, the rebellion of Wat Tyler, and
other romantic chapters in the history of the working
classes. It goes without saying that the party press
presented both ancient and modern history in a highly
colored form; conservatives were always represented as
villains and the champions of the poor as incapable of
wrong-doing. But at least such campaigns of education
gave a background to the agitation for the Charter,
supplied a sense of historical continuity with the popular
struggles of the past, and created a fraternal feeling for
the working classes in other countries.

The evidences of Chartist interest in the democratic
movements in continental Europe and in America are

numerous and striking; indeed, if the Chartist periodicals may be supposed to have had any influence on their readers, Chartism must have done more than any other factor to form the opinions of radical workingmen upon questions of foreign policy. But the degree of attention which the Chartists bestowed upon events in other countries was not constant, being very much greater after the revolutionary year of 1848 than it had ever been before. Such Chartist periodicals as *The English Republic, The Democratic Review, The Northern Tribune, The Red Republican, The Friend of the People, The National Instructor*, and other organs of the party in existence after 1848 gave as much or more space to the revolutions on the Continent than to the agitation for the Charter in England. In the years when the Chartist movement in England seemed nearest success and when the revolutionary movements in other European countries seemed far from being equally strong, the majority of Chartists confined their attention to the domestic situation. But even in those days not a few of the party leaders followed with the greatest sympathy the progress of democracy abroad. In 1844 William Lovett helped to organize the Association of Democratic Friends of All Nations,[1] and, in the same year, he supported a protest against the reception tendered by the British government to Nicholas I, Tsar of Russia.[2]

The Chartists were particularly interested in the nationalist movements in Italy, Hungary and Poland, and the Hungarian war for independence inspired almost as much enthusiasm as had the outbreak of the revolution in France. When the authority of the Habsburg

[1] Lovett, *Life and Struggles*, p. 307.
[2] *Ibid.*, pp. 297-9.

monarch had been restored in Hungary with the help
of Russia, the Chartists made heroes of the Hungarian
patriots and considered the rulers of Austria and Russia
as enemies of human liberty everywhere and therefore as
potential enemies of England. A typical Chartist ver-
dict grouped together Mazzini and Kossuth as "the two
highest models of political virtue existing."[1] Kossuth
was accorded a royal welcome by the workingmen of
Great Britain during his exile. Ernest Jones, however,
always more of an internationalist than a nationalist, did
not wish the Chartists to join the popular demonstrations until it became clear whether Kossuth was really a
champion of the poor and oppressed in all countries or
simply a brave warrior who cared only for his own land
and people. When Kossuth declared against Socialism,
Jones attacked him savagely in Notes to the People,[2]—
a course which probably cost Jones more friends than any
other act of his life, as Kossuth was still at the height
of his popularity.[3]

When the Austrian general Haynau, notorious for his
severity in crushing the revolutionists of Italy and Hungary, incautiously visited England in 1850, he met with a
very different reception from that which greeted Kossuth.
The Chartist weekly, The Red Republican, urged that he
be not permitted to land and that in case he did so there
should be "a manifestation of public opinion."[4] This
latter hope was gratified. The draymen of Barclay and
Perkins, brewers, attacked General Haynau with whips

[1] Cooper's Journal, Jan. 12, 1850.

[2] Notes to the People, vol. ii (1852), pp. 604–6.

[3] The Christian Socialist, Dec. 20, 1851, also expressed disappointment at Kossuth's anti-Socialist attitude, but in a much milder vein
than Ernest Jones.

[4] The Red Republican, Sept. 7, 1850.

202 THE DECLINE OF THE CHARTIST MOVEMENT [450

and sticks and forced him to flee for safety through the London streets. The Chartists were delighted by this episode[1] which so exactly met their expressed wishes, and the populace in general felt the same joy. The Russian government shared to the full the unpopularity of the Austrian, and some of the Chartists urged that England intervene to rescue Hungary from the combined armies of Austria and Russia, even if it meant a war with both countries.[2] It is probable that the Chartists, in spite of their declining influence with the British masses, did something to prepare them to welcome the Crimean war when it came as a war for European liberties against a pitiless oppressor.

The Chartists were unanimously anti-militarist in the sense that they disliked the heavy taxation necessary to keep up a large standing army, that they opposed all wars designed to extend the boundaries or the influence of the British Empire, and that they denounced especially every rumor of war with other nations whose political system was more or less tinctured with liberalism, such as France. But they never endorsed the principle of Cobden and Bright that England should never interfere in a European war that did not directly involve her own sovereignty and independence. As early as 1849 the Chartist journalist Thomas J. Wooler (writing under his pen-name of "The Black Dwarf") forecasted a coming war in which Turkey and England, perhaps with the aid of France, would be on one side and Austria and Russia on the other.[3] Except for the neutrality of Austria, as unexpected to most professional diplomats as it was to

---

[1] *The Red Republican*, Sept. 14, 1850.
[2] *The Democratic Review*, August, 1849.
[3] *The Plain Speakers*, Oct. 13, 1849.

the Chartists, this prediction exactly fitted the impending Crimean conflict. But the Chartists cared comparatively little for the issue of the integrity of the Ottoman Empire; their aim was rather the dismemberment of the anti-national Russian Empire. In 1853 W. J. Linton demanded "War with Russia. *Not in the Black Sea but in the Baltic,*"[1] and throughout 1854 *The Northern Tribune* urged an alliance with Poland.[2] After the war was ended, Ernest Jones denounced the British government for not having carried it on by an alliance with all the oppressed or menaced nationalities within the Russian Empire or at her boundaries, instead of acting solely on behalf of Turkey.[3]

The general attitude of the Chartists to foreign affairs presents many phases of interest. They knew the national aspirations of Italy very well, mainly through the personality of Joseph Mazzini, whose writings were printed or reprinted in several Chartist periodicals; they were familiar also with the wrongs of Hungary, Poland and Greece. But non-vocal nationalities which had not succeeded in getting their claims presented before the British public received little attention from the Chartists. An illuminating example of this is afforded by the "Map of Republican Europe" published in *The English Republic.*[4] There is no need to review in detail this Utopian map of Europe, except to note in passing how the best known nationalities were favored. Poland was made to extend from the Drina and the Dnieper rivers on the east to the Oder on the west, and from the Black Sea to

---

[1] *The English Republic*, Nov. 19, 1853; the italics are in the original.

[2] W. J. Linton and Thomas Cooper were the chief Chartist contributors to this periodical.

[3] *Evenings with the People.* Address of Jan. 27, 1857.

[4] *The English Republic*, May 22, 1854.

the Baltic; Bohemia and the Slavic parts of the Habsburg empire south of the Carpathians were annexed to Hungary; Macedonia, Albania and Constantinople went to Greece. Another peculiarity of the Chartist writings on foreign politics was their tendency to forget the different political needs and stages of development of different countries and to read all revolutionary movements elsewhere in the terms of the contemporary class struggle in England. For example, the Chartists tended to view all the moderate constitutional monarchists of Germany, Italy and other parts of continental Europe as enemies of the working class, and their projected reforms as "Whiggery." Few Chartists retained much interest in the French republic after the defeat of Louis Blanc and the "reds" and the resulting ascendancy of the bourgeoisie and the conservative peasantry; the establishment of the empire, while the Chartists unanimously deplored it, they regarded as of less moment than the closing of the national workshops.

The foreign country most admired by the Chartists, the nation which they most frequently compared with England to the disadvantage of the latter, was the United States of America. When the Chartist movement was strongest and the Chartist press most widely read and therefore most effective in forming public opinion, the diplomatic relations between the United States and Great Britain were far from cordial. The unsettled Maine boundary, the question of the ownership of the Oregon territory, the American sympathy shown to the Canadian rebels in 1837, the disputed fishing rights claimed by American citizens in the territorial waters of Canada, and other vexing issues which lay between the two governments, kept up an irritation that was greatly increased by the anti-American attitude of prominent English

writers and of the majority of upper-class newspapers
and periodicals. Chartist periodicals such as the *Power
of the Pence, English Chartist Circular* and many others,
labored faithfully to inspire in their readers the contrary sentiment of admiration for American institutions.
Chartists generally agreed with John Fielden's characterization of the founders of the American republic
as "the wisest men that as a body ever existed."[1] In
1849, during the height of the emigration movement,
Joseph Barker urged all who intended leaving England
to seek their homes in the United States rather than in
any British colony.[2] Barker followed his own advice and
filled many issues of *The People* with accounts of American conditions, which in the main were very favorable.

The Chartists valued the United States less for its
own sake than as a great experiment in political democracy, and they were quick to criticize what they considered the weak points of American civilization. Without
exception they disliked the "peculiar institution" of
chattel slavery and every act of the American government, such as the Mexican war, which tended to extend
or strengthen the slavery system. They discerned the
rise of industrialism and its attendant evils in the new
country and warned American democrats that their
political liberties would be endangered if the growth of
great fortunes were permitted to continue. *The National Instructor* published in 1850 a series of articles on
the land-reform movement in America, and many other
Chartist papers commended the land reformers and their
organ *Young America* as the hope of democracy in the
west.[3] But the very fear shown by the Chartists that

[1] Gammage, *History of the Chartist Movement*, p. 61.

[2] *The People*, vol. i, p. 121.

[3] Cf. *The Red Republican*, July 13, 1850; *Power of the Pence*, Nov.
11, 1848; *The Democratic Review*, June, 1849.

American institutions might fail was an index of their interest in the future of the country. When it is remembered that the writings and speeches of Radical and Chartist leaders were during the decade which preceded the American Civil War almost the sole source of the political opinions of the British working classes, it is scarcely surprising that they should have supported the cause of the preservation of that nation which they had been taught to consider the most important democracy in the world. The Lancashire operatives who were the chief sufferers from the blockade of Confederate ports which cut off the usual cotton shipments to England were, in spite of their material interest in a speedy restoration of peace, more consistent supporters of the cause of the North than any other considerable section of the British public, and they were also as a class the most closely associated with the Chartist movement and the most completely imbued with Chartist teachings.

Among the issues of the present day which are rooted in the activities of the Chartist period is the agitation for woman suffrage.[1] Whenever the Chartists spoke of "universal suffrage" or the followers of Sturge of "complete suffrage", manhood suffrage was invariably understood. Few of the party ever thought of applying the logic of democracy which they employed against other disqualifications for the franchise to the limitation based on sex. But the Chartist movement was none the less a potent factor in introducing working women to political life, for women bore a considerable share in the agitation for manhood suffrage. The report by Mr. Cripps in the House of Commons on the number

[1] On the general question of the position of women in the Chartis movement, see especially Schlüter, *Die Chartistenbewegung*, pp. 89 308

of signatures to the Chartist petition of 1848 contained the statement that " in every 100,000 names there were 8,200 women. "[1] The only particular importance attached to this finding at the time was that it weakened the case of the Chartists, because it meant that a very considerable proportion of those whom O'Connor and others had claimed as supporters of the petition would not be enfranchised even under the Charter. But to-day it is easy to see more than a negative significance in this remarkable proportion of women's signatures, since it served as measure of the interest which many English women had begun to take in the issues of public life.

The idea of suffrage as a right equally of men and of women, was probably rarely considered by the majority of the party, yet was not wholly foreign to the Chartist movement. William Lovett favored woman suffrage and had even contemplated introducing it into the Charter.[2] The plan was abandoned as too far in advance of the age to win favor, but, while the Chartist party never committed itself to equal suffrage, there was nothing to prevent individual members from urging it. Besides William Lovett, other prominent leaders, including John La Mont[3] and W. J. Linton,[4] believed in woman suffrage, and in 1842 a number of meetings of Chartist women passed resolutions favoring it.[5] It is impossible to say how much influence the equal suffragists of the party may have had in bringing the issue to public attention, for several decades were to elapse after the end of the Chartist movement before the suffrage question entered the

[1] *Hansard*, 3rd series, vol. xcviii, p. 290.
[2] Lovett, *Life and Struggles*, p. 170.
[3] *English Chartist Circular*, vol. ii, p. 111.
[4] *The English Republic*, Feb. 22, 1851.
[5] *Annual Register*, vol. lxxxiv, pp. 163-4; 187.

sphere of practical politics. At any rate they prepared
the minds of the classes associated with the Chartist
movement to consider equal suffrage as a possibility
when the time came for it to be more effectively agitated.

When the great wave of class discontent which we
call the Chartist movement had passed, the individuals
who had been associated with the movement as leaders
or as followers lost most of their importance for history.
Most of the Chartists became wholly absorbed in the life
of their trades-unions and co-operative societies and al-
lied themselves politically with the regular political parties, chiefly with the Radical wing of the Liberal party
captained at that time by John Bright. Some emigrated
to America or to Australia.[1] One by one the leaders
died off, emigrated, or deserted the party for other fields
of social service or political agitation. Henry Hetherington, Joseph Williams, Alexander Sharpe and others
of the party died during the cholera epidemic of 1849.[2]
John Fielden died in 1847; John Collins, Lovett's asso-
ciate, in 1850.[3] Feargus O'Connor died insane in 1855.
William Lovett continued to work in various causes of
reform and finally became the proprietor of the National
Hall in Holborn. Vincent became a lecturer. J. R.
Stephens returned to preaching at Ashton, and Richard
Oastler published a Tory democratic periodical which he
named "Altar, Throne and Cottage." McDouall emigrated to Australia. Reynolds continued as a radical
journalist. Julian Harney became secretary of a Republican Brotherhood, R. G. Gammage, the historian of the

[1] The Chartists who went to Australia took an active part in the democratic movements there and some of the old Chartist songs were long
familiar in the gold-mining districts. Schlüter, *op. cit.*, p. 349.

[2] Gammage, *op. cit.*, p. 349.

[3] *Ibid.*, pp. 401-2.

movement, of a Democratic Association. J. Bronterre
O'Brien lectured for the National Reform League.
Ernest Jones "outlived the Chartist era; lived to return
to peaceful agitation, to hold public controversy with . . .
Professor Blackie of Edinburgh, on the relative advantages of republicanism and monarchy, and to stand for a
Parliamentary borough at the general election of 1868;
and then his career was closed by death."[1] Thomas
Cooper, who lived till 1892, continued his literary activity
and also took up evangelistic work after being converted
from scepticism.[2] W. J. Linton, already well known as
a wood-engraver, devoted most of his attention to his
art, although he always retained his interest in social
and political reform. In 1866 he emigrated to America,
where he lived until his death in 1897.

There is a certain pathos in tracing the after careers
of these Chartist leaders. Several of them died in poverty, most of them sank out of sight among the crowd
of petty journalists and routine social workers, very
few attained such fame outside the movement as they
had known within it. Even more pathetic was the disappointment of a whole generation of working men and
women who were forced at last to resign themselves to
the continued existence of upper-class rule in the state
and to an indefinite postponement of the complete emancipation of their class in industry. But neither the officers nor the privates of the Chartist movement had
really fought in vain. They left the mind of England
changed,—perhaps the greatest of all possible revolutions.
The enfranchised classes had come to recognize the necessity for a continually expanding program of reform as

[1] J. McCarthy, *History of Our Own Times*, vol. ii, p. 17.
[2] *Life of Thomas Cooper, passim.*

the one method of preventing a violent and disastrous revolution. The unenfranchised classes had come to know themselves; to be conscious both of their strength and of their weakness. The very faults and blunders which wrecked Chartism have been turned to good account as a warning to later working-class movements. If the Chartist movement did not immediately obtain for England the Charter, at least it organized the people to make full use of democracy when it came.

BIBLIOGRAPHY.

Annual Register.

Ashworth, Henry. *The Preston Strike.* 1854.

Bamford, S. B. *Passages in the Life of a Radical.* 2 vols. London, 1844.

Bowley, Arthur L. *Wages in the United Kingdom in the Nineteenth Century.* Cambridge, 1900.

Brentano, Lujo. *Die Englische Chartistenbewegung. Preussische Jahrbücher.* Vol. 33. Berlin, 1874.

Bright, John, and Richardson, R. J. *A New Movement.* 1848.

Brougham, Lord Henry. *Reply to Lord John Russell's Letter to the Electors of Stroud.* London, 1839.

Carlyle, Thomas. *Chartism.* London, 1839.

Cooper, Thomas. *Life of Thomas Cooper.* Second Edition. London, 1872.

Dierlamm, Gotthilf. *Die Flugschriftenliteratur der Chartistenbewegung.* Naumburg, 1909.

Dolléans, E. *Le Chartisme.* 2 vols. Paris, 1912.

Eardley-Wilmot, John E. *A Letter to Lord Brougham.* 1857.

Engels, Friedrich. *Condition of the Working-Class in England in 1844.* Translated from the German. London, 1892. Original edition in 1845.

Frost, Thomas. *Forty Years' Recollections.* London, 1880.

Gammage, R. G. *History of the Chartist Movement.* Second edition. London, 1894.

Gonner, E. C. K. *Common Land and Inclosure.* London, 1912.

Hansard. *Parliamentary Debates.*

Hasbach, W. *History of the English Agricultural Labourer.* London, 1908.

Hayes, Carlton. *British Social Politics.* New York, 1913.

Holyoake, George J. *History of Coöperation in England.* 2 vols. London, 1879.

———. *History of Coöperation in Rochdale.* Seventh edition. 1872.

———. *Life and Character of Henry Hetherington.* London, 1849.

———. *Sixty Years of an Agitator's Life.* Fourth edition. 2 vols. London, 1900.

Howell, G. *Labour Legislation, Labour Movements and Labour Leaders.* New York, 1902.

Huber, V. A. *Ueber die coöperativen Arbeiterassociationen in England.* 1852.

Hutchins, B. L., and Harrison, A. (Mrs. F. H. Spencer). *A History of Factory Legislation.* London, 1911.

Hyndman, H. M. *The Historical Basis of Socialism in Englanl.* London, 1883.

Ingestre, Viscount (Chas. John Shrewsbury). *Meliora.* 2 vols. London, 1852-3.

Jones, Edward D. *Chartism—A Chapter in English Industrial History.* Wisconsin Academy of Sciences, Arts and Letters. Vol. 12. December, 1898.

Jones, Ernest. *Chartist Songs and Fugitive Pieces.* London, undated.
———. *Evenings with the People.* Published lectures. 1856-7.

Jones, Lloyd, and Ludlow, J. M. *The Progress of the Working Class.* London, 1867.

Kay, Joseph. *The Social Condition and the Education of the People in England and Europe.* 2 vols. 1850.

Kingsley, Charles. *Alton Locke, Tailor and Poet.* 1850.
———. *The Application of Associative Principles and Methods to Agriculture.* 1851.
———. *Who Are the Friends of Order?* 1852.

Lester, C. Edwards. *The Condition and Fate of England.* 2 vols. New York, 1842.

Letter from one of the Special Constables in London. Anonymous. 1848.

Lovett, William. *Life and Struggles in Pursuit of Bread, Knowledge, and Freedom.* London, 1876.
———. *Social and Political Morality.* London, 1853.

Lovett, William, and Collins, John. *Chartism.* Second edition. London, 1841.

Ludlow, J. M. *The Master Engineers and their Workmen.* 1852.

Martineau, Harriet. *A History of the Thirty Years' Peace.* 4 vols. London, 1877. Original edition in 1851.

McCarthy, Justin. *History of Our Own Times.* 4 vols. London, 1880.

Memoranda of the Chartist Agitation in Dundee. Anonymous; undated.

Miall, Edward. *The Suffrage.* 1848.

Molesworth, W. M. *A History of England from the Year 1830.* 3 vols. London, 1872.

Morley, John. *Life of Richard Cobden.* London, 1881.

Nadaud, M. *Histoire des Classes ouvrières en Angleterre.* Paris, 1872.

National Reform Tract. Number 5. *To the Distressed Classes.* 1855.

Neale, Edward Vansittart. *May I Not Do What I Will with My Own?* 1852.

Nicholls, G. *History of the English Poor Law.* 2 vols. London, 1898.

O'Brien, J. Bronterre. *Labour's Wrongs and Labour's Remedy.* Undated pamphlet.

————. *Propositions of the National Reform League for the Peaceful
Regeneration of Society.* 1850.

————. *The Rise, Progress and Phases of Human Slavery.* London,
1885. Original edition in 1850.

O'Connor, Feargus. *A Practical Work on the Management of Small
Farms.* 1843.

————. Published report of the *Trial of Feargus O'Connor and Fifty-
eight Others at Lancaster.* 1843.

Parliamentary Accounts and Papers.

Parliamentary Reports.

People's Charter, The. London, 1832. Anonymous abstract from *The
Rights of Nations.*

Periodicals :

  Blackwood's Magazine.
  Bronterre's National Reformer.
  Bury Times.
  Chartist Circular.
  The Christian Socialist.
  Cooper's Journal.
  The Democratic Review.
  Edinburgh Review.
  English Chartist Circular.
  The English Republic.
  The Friend of the People.
  The Labourer.
  McDouall's Chartist and Republican Journal.
  National Instructor.
  National Reformer and Manx Weekly Review.
  The Nonconformist.
  Northern Star.
  Northern Tribune.
  Notes to the People.
  The People.
  The Plain Speaker.
  Power of the Pence.
  The Red Republican.
  The Reformer's Almanac.
  Reformer's Companion to the Almanac.
  The Republican.
  Times.
  The Vanguard.
  The Weekly Adviser and Artizan's Companion.

Porter, G. R. *The Progress of the Nation.* Revised by F. W. Hirst. London, 1912.

Prentice, Archibald. *A History of the Anti-Corn Law League.* 2 vols. London, 1853.

Prothero, Rowland E. *English Farming Past and Present.* London, 1912.

The Radical Reformers of England, Scotland and Wales to the Irish People. Anonymous; undated.

Report of the Proceedings at the Conference of Delegates of the Middle and Working Classes, held at Birmingham, April 5, 1842, and three following days. London, 1842.

Report of the Sixth Annual Conference of the National Association of United Trades. 1850.

Representation of the Case of the Executive Committee of the Central Association of Employers of Operative Engineers. 1852.

Revolutionary Rhymes and Songs for Socialists. 1886.

Richard, Henry. *Memoirs of Joseph Sturge.* 1864.

Right and Expediency of Universal Suffrage. Anonymous; undated.

Rose, J. Holland. *The Rise of Democracy.* London, 1897.

Russell, Lord John. *Letter to the Electors of Stroud.* London, 1839.

Schlüter, Hermann. *Die Chartisten-Bewegung.* New York, 1916.

Schlüter, Hermann. *Die Chartistenbewegung in England. Sozial-Demokratische Bibliothek.* Vol. 16. Zürich, 1887.

Slaney, R. A. *A Plea for the Working Classes.* 1847.

Slater, Gilbert. *The Making of Modern England.* London, 1913.

———. *Report of the Land Enquiry Committee.* Vol. 1. London, 1913.

Solly, Henry. *James Woodford, Carpenter and Chartist.* 2 vols. London, 1881.

———. *What Says Christianity to the Present Crisis?* 1842.

Styles, T. *The Coming Era.* 1848.

Tildsley, John L. *Die Entstehung und die Okonomischen Grundsätze der Chartistenbewegung.* Jena, 1898.

Toynbee, Arnold. *Lectures on the Industrial Revolution in England.* London, 1884.

Traill, H. D. *Social England.* 6 vols. London, 1899.

Trevelyan, George M. *The Life of John Bright.* London, 1914.

Wallas, Graham. *Life of Francis Place.* London, 1898.

Watkins, John. *Impeachment of Feargus O'Connor.* 1843.

Webb, Sidney, and Webb, Beatrice. *The History of Trade Unionism.* London, 1911.

Wood, George Henry. *The History of Wages in the Cotton Trade.* London, 1910.

Woodworth, Arthur V. *Christian Socialism in England.* London, 1903.

INDEX

463]

VITA

The author of the foregoing study was born September 2, 1892 at Laramie, Wyoming. He received his elementary education in the public schools of Laramie and of New York City, and prepared for college at the De Witt Clinton High School. In June 1912 he received from Columbia College the degree of Bachelor of Science with highest honors in modern history, chemistry and English literature. In 1913 he received the degree of Master of Arts in the Faculty of Political Science of Columbia University, and has since acted as assistant in history in Columbia College and in the extension work of the University. In the departments of History and of Economics he has taken courses under Professors James T. Shotwell, James Harvey Robinson, F. H. Giddings, W. R. Shepherd, W. M. Sloane, W. A. Dunning, V. G. Simkhovitch, R. E. Chaddock, K. F. T. Rathgen, Dr. B. M. Anderson and Mr. R. R. Hill and has attended the seminar of Professor Shotwell. In 1914 he published *Fated or Free*, a philosophical dialog, and in 1915 *Peace with Honor*, an historical pamphlet.